BONSAI

CULTURE AND CARE OF MINIATURE TREES

By the Sunset Editorial Staff
Book Editor: Jack McDowell

LANE BOOKS • MENLO PARK, CALIF.

Photographers

William Aplin: 22 (top), 50, 67, 69, 72, 73. Aplin-Dudley Studio: 49 (left), 59, 60. Ernest Braun: 76 (right). Carroll C. Calkins: 13. Clyde Childress: 5, 18 (top). Glenn M. Christiansen: 17 (bottom right), 43, 46, 54, 58. Robert Cox: 18 (bottom), 29 (middle). Dick Dawson: 70. Don Erskine: 53. Jeannette Grossman: 17 (top left). R. L. Hudson: 42 (top). Art Hupy: 42 (middle, bottom). Tatsuo Ishimoto: 7 (bottom), 15, 24 (bottom), 34 (left), 66 (right). Roy Krell: 71 (left). Jack McDowell: 8, 10, 17 (top right, bottom left), 29 (top, bottom), 32 (top), 34 (right), 35, 49 (right), 56, 64 (right), 65, 66 (left). Ken Molino: 39. Virginia Moore: 7 (middle), 12 (left), 20, 27, 32 (bottom), 38 (right), 40, 74. Don Normark: 6, 33, Marjorie Ray Piper: 12 (right). John Robinson: 14, 64 (left). Blair Stapp: 1, 7 (top), 24 (top). Darrow M. Watt: 11, 21, 26, 37, 48, 52, 61, 63, 71 (right), 76 (left).

Cover photo by Robert Cox

The tree silhouettes illustrating bonsai growth habits, shown on pages 30 and 31, and the silhouette on the Contents page, page 3, were made, with modifications, from photographs appearing in the book, *The Japanese Art of Miniature Trees and Landscapes*, by Yuju Yoshimura, published by Charles E. Tuttle Co., Inc., Rutland, Vermont, and Tokyo.

Eleventh Printing February 1971

Contents

Bonsai...A Corner of the World

Fads and fashions rise and fall with the regularity of the tides, and each day brings either a new fancy or renewed interest in an old one. The rubber plant, the fern, the aspidistra that graced grandmother's living room fell into early disfavor in our functional, modern homes, then underwent a revival as a way of bringing a bit of natural greenery indoors.

The Japanese are less quixotic. For centuries they have striven to keep nature in and about the house and so have developed many means that would answer this need as well as prevail as stabilizing influences. Bonsai—miniature potted trees—have been one answer.

Whether you approach bonsai as an art or a hobby, they are a way of enjoying nature and having it near at hand. Bonsai represent a corner of the world—a high mountainside, perhaps an alpine meadow—captured as if by magic at a perfect moment and kept alive in an impossibly shallow container. Fortunately, the wisdom of the Orient is not a prerequisite for their enjoyment, and the magic is no more than common sense garden practice.

There are many ways you can create bonsai, and caring for them is no small part of the pleasure of ownership. Most of the delight derives from seeing nature at work on a small scale in your home or garden.

The autumn of leaves.
Even the potted trees are
Not inviolate.

*The Japanese started it all.
A few centuries ago they began collecting
trees that had been dwarfed by nature.
Collecting developed into cultivating,
East eventually met West, and today bonsai
(pronounce it bone-sigh, with the accent at the
end) culture is an art practiced the world over.
Most of the mysteries surrounding this ancient
craft turn out to be common-sense gardening
practices, and many of its specialized methods
can be applied rewardingly in several other
areas of green thumbery.*

East or West, bonsai brings far corners of the world into your home. A few of the many possible styles are shown above.

The World in Miniature

ON SEEING A BONSAI for the first time, one man shook his head and said, "I just don't believe it."

If you were told what a bonsai is, you too might find it difficult to believe. And if you were to see a 300-year-old tree a foot high growing happily in a couple of inches of soil, you could be excused for doubting even your eyes. There is something incredible, something magical about a bonsai. And yet, all of the magic and the mystery is but the result of one thing — an understanding of plant growth habits.

Persons viewing a good specimen invariably, after their initial surprise, associate the tiny thing with Japan. There seems to be something typically Oriental about such a tree. Without having to be told, we instinctively feel what bonsai is, what it symbolizes — a portion of the world in miniature.

Japan itself is a relatively small country. For most of its recorded history it has been heavily populated. Virtually every inch of available land is settled or under intensive cultivation. There are few places where a person can get away from all other people for very long. The most remote countryside is never long without a troupe of charming but chattering school children or a friendly but inquisitive hiker.

Japan is also a country with great natural beauty. It is a land of rugged mountains, of sparkling coastlines, of island-studded inland seas. Being everywhere close to the mountains and to the ocean, the Japanese place great value on nature. They know how to see harmony and beauty in all of her ways.

To bring this beauty even nearer, the Japanese have perfected the fine art of duplicating nature in many

Nice mixture of nature and the hand of man is shown in this simulated wildlife scene. Weeping deodar (*Cedrus deodara* 'Pendula') is trained in a natural manner against the large boulders. Same tree is often used for cascaded bonsai form.

forms. They have achieved this by learning to know how and why nature does certain things.

A small Japanese garden creates for enjoyment an illusion of many miles of forest, or mountain slope, or seacoast. It invites even the most casual observer. A *sumi* brush painting — usually of some natural subject — is purposely left incomplete. What is *not* there requires of the viewer a certain amount of mental participation. A bonsai is a tiny corner of the world that is meant to be enjoyed in itself as well as for what it represents.

Through bonsai, the city dweller, who daily sees concrete and steel, can have a bit of greenery to himself. Though enclosed by four walls, he can escape in his imagination into a natural world that exists in his little trees. For a few minutes, walls can be made to vanish, an inch-high mound of moss can become a green meadow, a small rock a mountainside, a few seedlings an entire forest. This is the magic of bonsai.

Bringing Nature Home

The earliest bonsai (literally, "tray trees") were not known by that name, nor were they deliberate attempts to actually dwarf a plant. The origins of bonsai as an art are somewhat murky, but it is fairly certain that as long as 500 years ago people in Japan were collecting and potting trees that had been distorted by winds or stunted through poor natural conditions. Little thought was given to any training of such plants, since in their rugged, natural forms they represented a landscape in which the owner could see a portion of the world.

In a very few years, owing to the great numbers of people tramping through the wilds in search of them, naturally stunted trees became scarce. As a matter of fact, the Japanese landscape was in real danger of becoming denuded by appreciative but overly numerous collectors.

It is a credit to the art, and to the Japanese intellect, that bonsai was not dropped as a passing fad. Realizing that there were not enough trees on their islands to supply the wants of everyone, the Japanese turned from collecting to propagating. They tried growing small conifers in containers — from seed, from cuttings, and from graftings. They gave little thought at first to any training. The trees were allowed to take their own natural shape, but were kept confined. This is still a simple and satisfying way to get a good-looking small-scale tree.

Then one day some bold soul, whose identity has long been lost to history, snipped off a branch or twisted a twig — perhaps accidentally, or maybe to get it out of the way — and the art of bonsai was born.

Although it took a bit more time, a bit more care, the practice of *cultivating* a dwarf tree, rather than collecting it from the wild, became more popular and certainly more practical. The results were not as immediate, but cultivating made expeditions into the wilds unnecessary and assured a specimen without the attendant danger of broken limbs.

Later in this book you will learn of the simplest method of obtaining a bonsai. The most nondescript nursery plant can easily be transformed into a charming subject merely by pruning and potting. Nursery cans may not have been in use in Japan way back then, but the idea was the same.

Since the aim of bonsai is the reproduction of nature, the trees and their formation must follow nature's ways. Some stores and gift shops sell artificial miniature trees made from wood, plastic, paper, and wire, or even kits of such materials for building your own. These often go under the name of "Ming Trees," or, worse yet, "Bonsai Trees." Such things, of course, are not bonsai, since the essence of a bonsai is its reality as a living plant.

Nature is copied, true. But much of the pleasure in this art lies in successfully duplicating natural forms with other natural forms.

Bonsai East and West

Bonsai culture is not new in the United States. American citizens of Japanese descent have been raising such plants here, particularly on the West Coast, for more than thirty years. However, it has been only since around 1950 that the interest of Americans has been aroused and they have taken to this most enjoyable pastime.

Like many hobbies, bonsai culture is relaxing in that it represents a complete change of pace for anyone, regardless of profession or of other interests. Some of the most enthusiastic practitioners are gardeners and nurserymen, who, in spite of their daily work with plants, often spend evenings and weekends caring for their dwarf trees.

This is not to say that such trees require a great deal of care. Quite the contrary. Aside from the occasional training time, they require a minimum of attention other than watering.

Little room is required. A sheltered window ledge can hold a small collection of bonsai, and a folding card table will serve as a temporary work center. Apartment dwellers and persons living in retirement homes can enjoy this hobby fully as much as the owner of a multi-acre estate.

The cost is minimal. Of course, as with any other hobby, you put as many dollars into it as you wish. But you can derive just as much enjoyment, and probably expend less effort, with a minimum investment. How much is a minimum investment? A start

Cotoneaster is covered with cheery white flowers in the spring and orange-red berries in the fall. In America it is a very popular bonsai subject.

Imported from Japan when it was fifty years old, this Japanese black pine was an attraction at Panama Pacific Exposition held in San Francisco in 1915.

Rugged as an aged mountain-grown tree, this bonsai (a 4-year-old *Juniperus procumbens*) was potted in the low bonsai container from a one-gallon can.

With fragrant white blossoms, small leaves, textured wood, the star jasmine *(Trachelospermum jasminoides)* makes an ideal bonsai. This 20-year-old specimen is 18 inches high, puts on best show in late spring. Container is brown, unglazed.

into the hobby could be made for $5.00, maybe even a little less. This would buy a nursery plant, a container, and a couple of the most basic tools. The remaining equipment can easily be found around the house, and reasonably good garden soil can be obtained almost anywhere.

Perhaps it is because of this very simplicity that bonsai can become habit forming. More than one person has started out with absolutely no knowledge, but with the interest to "try it with just one plant," and before long has found his enthusiasm uncontrollable and his collection enlarging. That's the way with bonsai. One plant, say an upright evergreen, is joined by another, perhaps a clump of maples, then a cascaded wisteria is added. Before long the collection has grown and the collector's interest has grown and he finds that he is looking for excuses to somehow get to his specimens every day.

So much mumbo jumbo has been written about the art of bonsai — both by experts and by completely unqualified novices — that it seems to many newcomers a great mystery whose understanding requires the wisdom of the Orient as well as its cultural heritage. This is indeed unfortunate because miniature tree culture is no more mysterious than vegetable gardening.

If a person wishes to follow tradition to the letter and make a full-time occupation of raising bonsai, he can very easily become embroiled in a myriad of details and spend all of his time at it. On the other hand, the person with but a few minutes a week can lose himself during those times in a very pleasurable manner.

Aside from several very basic considerations that are common to all living plants, there are few if any real rules. What is necessary, however, is an attitude of patience. You shouldn't expect results overnight. That is, you shouldn't expect to have in a week or a month, or even in several months, a handsome flowering tree, or a tree that bears peaches or cherries furiously. Bonsai takes very little time and effort, but it does take some patience.

Bonsai purists say that only true species are worthy of consideration — that dwarf forms of a species should not be cultivated as bonsai or called such. They feel that somehow it's cheating to begin with dwarf stock to make a miniature tree.

This is a rule that can be bent — or ignored. If you think you can make a pleasing bonsai from dwarf plant stock and enjoy trying, go ahead and do it. The tree shown on page 66 is a dwarf pomegranate (*Punica granatum* 'Nana'); even though the plant is a dwarf to begin with, who is to say it's not a good bonsai?

Must a Bonsai Be Old?

One of the first disparities that strikes someone who has had his interest aroused in bonsai is the age — or apparent age — of the trees. At any show or display there are antiques 100 years old, 200 years old, perhaps even older. And anyone who enjoys this hobby, and who has collected bonsai for any length of time, will have in his collection trees that may range in age from 10 years to 100 years or more.

Does this mean that such trees have been under culture all those years? Does it mean that a lifetime, or several lifetimes, of care is necessary in order to create a handsome tree?

Not at all. A bonsai may very well be a hundred years old, but this doesn't mean that exactly 100 years ago someone planted the seed from which it grew. Nor does it mean that the plant has been under cultivation all that time. Many bonsai of apparent great age have spent the greater part of their life in the wild, growing in a natural state before being collected and trained for container life. See, for example, some of the specimens illustrated in later pages whose captions note total age as well as number of years in a container.

A question commonly asked is: Must a bonsai be really old? Again, not at all. What is important is not the actual age of a tree, but its apparent age. This is where bonsai offers a fascinating challenge. Making a three-year-old pine that is a foot tall look like a 50-year-old pine that is 40 feet tall is a most satisfying pastime.

Of course, the older a bonsai is, no matter what its origin, the more valuable it is, simply for the reason that considerable time and effort have been put into its care.

The impression of age and of reality is achieved through careful observation of mature trees in nature. You should make it a habit to study various types of trees of various ages that are growing under a variety of natural conditions. Try to determine what combination of physical factors makes a tree just what it is. Then duplicate those factors — by planting, trimming, wiring, as shown in this book — to create in miniature an aged tree.

At the bottom of page 7 is a bonsai juniper. Without reading the caption, cover the container with your hand and imagine this plant as a fully grown tree living in the wild. As a tree it could have struggled for existence on a mountainside. In its natural state, such a tree might be 20 feet tall and perhaps 70 years old. Now take your hand away from the container to restore the scale. The actual height of the plant is less than a foot. Its total age, when the photo was taken, was about four years. It began life as a bonsai less than a year before it was photographed.

Now look at the juniper on this page. This tree, though about twice as high as the other, is more than 100 years old. It had grown in the wild for many years before being gathered for container life. Evergreen conifers are one of the favorite bonsai subjects because even when very young they give an impression of great age.

Determining the real age of a bonsai is pretty much a matter of guesswork. If a tree dies, you can bisect the trunk and count the growth rings. This will enable you to talk about how old the tree *was*. True age is not of great importance. However, if you absolutely must know how old a bonsai is, you can use a small increment borer. This is a cutting device that enables you to take a tiny core from the trunk of a tree without damage. You then inspect the core and count the rings. Such necessarily small borers are not easy to come by. Check a scientific equipment supply house or mail order garden supply catalogs. After making such a hole, be sure to plug it with grafting wax to keep insects and diseases from attacking the tree.

Training in the Bonsai Manner

Although they are not to be considered bonsai, the form of many garden growing shrubs and trees will be enhanced by shaping and training in the bonsai style. For example, rather than letting a particular species of juniper develop its own characteristic form, why not try pruning it heavily to let a little light and air through and to expose a few of the limbs. This will give it much more personality than if it were allowed to grow naturally.

Even though growing in the ground, with an extensive root system, most plants can take this kind of treatment. Moreover, they will respond to it with richer growth. In addition to utilizing pruning to give a bonsai character to a plant, you can wire and bend

Real age is evident in this two-hundred-year-old Western juniper gathered from wild, even though tree is less than two feet tall. Container is unglazed.

branches to give form to what might otherwise be an ordinary shrub or tree.

Large container plants can gain considerable personality through application of bonsai methods. They become, in effect, giant bonsai.

You can make almost any kind of a plant into a reasonably good looking bonsai. Of course, there are species that lend themselves better to certain treatments or styles, and some plants must have their basic growth habits modified considerably. Though a few trees are classical favorites — pines, maples, oaks — there is no reason why others can't be cultivated in this manner. Even herbs, such as oregano and rosemary, make handsome bonsai.

Remember that bonsai culture is not a discipline with rigid procedures that must be strictly followed. Some of the methods are tried and true. Others are one of many means to the same end. Don't be hesitant about departing even from tradition and attempting something different. More important than techniques and their result is your enjoyment.

Bonsai are obtained from many places and in many ways, none of them too devious for the enthusiast. To be historically correct you should brave the wild to collect your stunted trees. However, you can also find potential bonsai waiting your touch in nursery cans or you can easily propagate them by any of at least seven methods. The choice is yours. And if you should decide to import an aged tree, there are a few things you might like to know . . .

Bonsai are very special plants, but most means of propagating them, as by cuttings, are regular garden practice.

Where Do They Come From?

THE BONSAI ENTHUSIAST in the Western United States is indeed fortunate. He enjoys an equable climate in most areas for most of the year. He has a wide variety of native plants to choose from. He has, close-at-hand, enthusiasts of Japanese descent who have been instrumental in popularizing the hobby. All of these factors combine in giving him a variety of methods to choose from in obtaining bonsai material.

Some species are more commonly used than others for bonsai. Nevertheless, you may safely commit to memory the following axiom: *Almost any kind of woody plant material can be made into an attractive looking bonsai.* Of course, some plants are difficult to dwarf because they don't take kindly to being contained in a pot, no matter how handsome the pot may be. Even though specific plants are mentioned from time to time in this book, or in other books, don't be

timid about experimenting with others. If you fail, try something new, or try the same species again, in a different way. One time you'll hit on the right combination that will make a plant into a good bonsai.

A great deal of the pleasure in working with bonsai lies in achieving something that no one else has been able to accomplish. Most professionals agree that eucalypts cannot be container grown. Many growers share the opinion that palms don't look well as bonsai. If you take such statements at face value, you'll never know otherwise. By testing them, you'll find out for yourself whether they are fact or personal opinion. This is one area of gardening where you should feel free of rules and standard procedures. Just because something has never been done before is no reason why it can't be done now, or tomorrow, or the next day.

The Makings of a Tree

At least in the beginning you'll probably do better working with the more common bonsai plants. Most of them are available at nurseries, and most of them will take abuses that wouldn't be tolerated by other plants. The following categories and recommendations are, of course, arbitrary. Many species that have been put into one group will certainly go just as well in another, and many, many plants not shown here, for the sake of simplicity, can be substituted for others. For other listings see pages 30, 31, 78, 79.

Good Plants for the Beginner. Firethorn (*Pyracantha coccinea* or *P. fortuneana*): Small leaves; evergreen; red or orange berries in autumn; recovers from over-pruning; branches bend easily. Cotoneaster (*C. dammeri, C. conspicua* 'Decora', or *C. microphylla*)*:* Characteristics similar to those for firethorn. Dwarf pomegranate (*Punica granatum* 'Nana'): Deciduous; twiggy branches; tiny green leaves; red flowers and fruits. Juniper (*Juniperus scopulorum* or *J. virginiana*): Hardy evergreen; heavy foliage takes to pruning; wide variety of forms.

Old Favorites. The following plants make especially good looking bonsai. Many of them are favorite classical subjects. Sargent juniper (*Juniperus chinensis sargentii*); graybark elm or sawleaf zelkova (*Z. serrata*)*;* Japanese black pine (*Pinus thunbergii*)*;* flowering cherries (*Prunus subhirtella, P. yedoensis*); wisteria (*Wisteria floribunda, W. sinensis*); Kurume azaleas; Hinoki cypress (*Chamaecyparis obtusa*).

Specialized Plants. In addition to the more common plants noted here, and shown in photographs throughout this book, certain plants that are native to certain geographical areas and climates make fine bonsai. The few following, though somewhat specialized, may be available in your area. If so, they are worth a try. In Hawaii successful bonsai have been made from the Queensland umbrella tree (*Brassaia actinophylla*), Japanese black pine (*Pinus thunbergii*), banyan (*Ficus bengalensis*), royal poinciana (*Delonix regia*), bougainvillea, Surinam cherry (*Eugenia uniflora*), ironwood (*Casuarina*, various species). In the Pacific Northwest some growers have done quite well with mountain hemlock (*Tsuga mertensiana*), alpine fir (*Abies lasiocarpa*), white bark pine (*Pinus albicaulis*), Engelmann spruce (*Picea engelmannii*).

American hornbeam (*Carpinus caroliniana*) is partially deciduous, has shiny orange and red foliage. This upright specimen came from a gallon nursery can.

Oregano is fairly uncommon as bonsai material, but like a few other woody herbs (rosemary, sage, wormwood), it can easily be trained into a miniature tree.

Bonsai country can be anywhere. Form of the wind-blown pine shown above is typical of trees growing on mountain sides. In the vicinity of such mature trees you are sure to find many small specimens that have been dwarfed by nature.

For various reasons, some plants don't adapt well to life as bonsai. A few don't take to having their roots confined; some are too-vigorous growing. However, why not accept the challenge and see if you can get anywhere with any of the following that may be available in your area.

Western red cedar or giant arborvitae (*Thuja plicata*), American mountain ash (*Sorbus americana*), madrone (*Arbutus menziesii* — seems to need more root room than it can find in a container), Rangpur lime (*Citrus aurantifolia* 'Rangpur' — won't last with overwatering), Chinese pistache (*Pistacia chinensis* — unpredictable; may take to container life, may not), manzanita (*Arctostaphylos manzanita* and other species — a handsome, gnarled shrub in wild, usually doesn't survive long as a bonsai).

Gather Specimens if You're Hardy

Most of the very old bonsai you may see have spent most of their life in natural surroundings, growing in the earth or in cracks in rocks. Through the years they lived in the wild they were exposed to all manner of climatic extremes and physical abuses. Many of them have gone through a real struggle for existence.

Such plants make the best bonsai. They have developed a form that speaks of their environment; they look old (often older than they actually are); they have become adapted to surviving under adverse conditions. When such plants are put into a container, they invariably outshine any other specimens that may be around them.

Small and scraggy, this juniper seemed to be a natural bonsai when gathered from high mountain elevations. Estimated age is 50 years; height is 21 inches.

It would seem a simple matter to go into the wild and dig out such a plant, bring it home and pot it, then sit back and enjoy it. As simple as all this might seem, however, there are a few points that should be observed before, during, and after collecting natural specimens.

What you should know

The best time for collecting plants in the wild is generally during March or April. During these months, over most of the country, new growth or leaves have not yet begun to sprout and the plants will feel a minimum of shock in being uprooted and transferred to a different environment.

After sprouting has started, new leaves are easily damaged, and the sudden shock of being dug up will usually not be tolerated. Before these months, most plants are dormant, and disturbed root systems usually won't be able to re-establish themselves.

What you should take

On a collecting trip you can load yourself with enough equipment to supply an exploration team to the top of Mount Everest, or you can simplify the items and still have a good chance at bringing back a specimen that will survive. Below are listed the minimum tools. You can add to these if you wish; perhaps you'll find you can get along with even less.

Small shovel. The collapsible Army type is best. It's little, and you'll have to dig more than you would with a big one, but it's lightweight and has a sharp end.

Some polyethylene sheeting and stout string, for wrapping root balls.

Sphagnum moss, for packing around the root ball.

Container of water, for wetting leaves and root ball.

Small pry bar, for getting roots out of rocks.

How to do it

Wherever you hope to collect a specimen, be sure to obtain a permit or permission from the owner of the land. If the land is private, explain just what you want to do, emphasizing that you are interested only in small, distorted trees. Often the owner will be glad to have such "misfits" off his land. Leave the property in neat order—don't fail to fill holes you make in digging up plants. If the area is in a National Park or on Government land, chances are that you won't be able to gather any specimens.

Once you find the tree you want, dig it up carefully without injuring the taproot. Get as large a ball of earth around the roots as possible. If the tree is growing out of a rock, you may have to do a little work with the pry bar.

Cover the roots and the earth with wet sphagnum, peat moss, or similar material, then wrap the ball in polyethylene film and tie it securely. In transporting the plant, secure it, in order that it won't roll about and damage its branches. Sprinkle the branches (or foliage, if it's an evergreen) with water every few hours.

As soon as you get home, plant the tree in deep, damp sawdust or in loose garden soil. Unwrap the root ball, but don't let the earth fall away from the roots. Spray the tree well, and keep it out of direct sun and wind.

After several months, new roots will start to form, and you can be fairly sure your specimen will survive. However, don't take it up and put it into a pot yet. Keep it watered, and start feeding it.

After a year, the tree will be ready to be dug up. If there are a great many fine roots around the base, you can cut some of these back to fit the tree into its container. If the plant has a taproot, do not cut it short. Remove about a fourth of it, then in a year take off a little more, and in the third year remove it entirely.

In potting a collected tree for the first time, you can prune the branches lightly if shaping is necessary.

After the tree has been in a container for a full year (two years after collecting) it can be started on a regular training program, if such is needed. Often, a tree collected in the wild will not need any wiring or shaping for several years.

Obtaining bonsai by collecting is not at all difficult, but it is a long-term proposition. Except for watering and feeding during the first year, the tree should be left strictly alone. Heavy pruning, or digging it up "just to have a peek at the roots," can be fatal.

A Shortcut... The Nursery Plant

The easiest method for obtaining bonsai — and the one most recommended for the novice — is adapting nursery stock. Nurseries have a wide variety of plants, and your nurseryman can fill you in on a particular specimen's growth habits. Plants in 1- to 5-gallon cans have been essentially in training pots for some time in that their root systems have become adapted to cramped conditions.

Look for the castoff

In looking for a potential bonsai, watch for the plant with a twisted or dwarf-like character. Inspect the plant from the ground up. Push back the foliage and

Two potential bonsai subjects that were picked out after a few minutes of browsing in a nursery. Below you see how these same plants were shaped and planted.

This nursery-can azalea shows good bonsai form when planted away from center of glazed container. "Tree" is slanted for balance and for added interest.

Daphne, larger of the two plants shown here, came from a five-gallon nursery can. Foliage was thinned out just enough to show the basic branch structure.

look at the base structure on several sides. A multi-trunk structure may be desirable, or side trunks can be cut off when the plant is put into a container.

Another way to get a good look at the trunk structure is to up-end the can and give it a couple of knocks to slide the root ball to the top of the can. This doesn't harm the plant, and you don't have to worry about the nurseryman charging down on you for damaging his stock.

Watch for plants with small leaves, with a heavy, thick, or twisted trunk, and with an open branching system or one that is full enough that it can be pruned and shaped into interesting forms. Look for large roots that protrude above the soil in the can. Although this is sometimes a sign of the plant being potbound, such roots add a great deal of character to a bonsai.

Getting it home

After you've chosen your tree, don't let the nurseryman cut the can unless you expect to repot the plant immediately. When cans are cut, roots dry out fast.

Don't expect to chop back enormous amounts of roots all at one time to get a canned tree into a small bonsai container. Chances are that the plant won't survive such brutal treatment. Instead, thin back the root ball by a third and put the tree into a container slightly smaller than the one you took it from. In eight months or so, thin the roots some more and transfer the tree to a still smaller container. By working at it in a progressive manner, you'll be able to get the root system safely down to whatever size you need without the danger of losing the plant.

The fine details of transferring a plant from a nursery can to a bonsai container are given in the chapter titled "A Certain Amount of Care."

From Seed or Seedling

If you are blessed with patience, and enjoy seeing a plant develop from next to nothing, try raising a bonsai from seed or from a seedling. There's a great deal of pleasure in watching the early development of a plant, and you'll have complete control over its shape.

Seedlings are available at many nurseries. Some mail order companies specialize in seeds and seedlings for bonsai culture. Being such small items, they are quite economical to ship and usually are not disturbed by travel.

Plant a seed

In sowing seeds, spread granular soil in the bottom of a wooden flat, then add a layer of regular soil.

When sowing seeds, plant more than you'll need. Not all of them will germinate, and those that do sprout can be thinned to give you the choicest plants. Larger seeds (see below) can be poked into the soil with a finger. They can be started directly in pots, paper containers, or plant bands. Put two or three seeds in each, then thin to the strongest seedling.

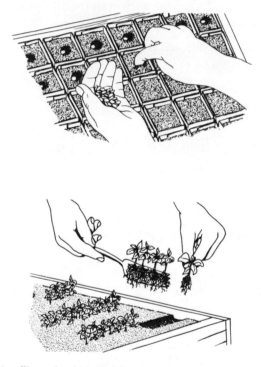

Seedlings should be pricked out as soon as possible after they have two sets of leaves. Seedlings are delicate, so be careful not to injure tender stems or roots. If seedlings come out with roots entangled, separate them, as shown below, by soaking root ball in water. Work rapidly and in the shade, and keep roots away from drying winds or drafts.

Laceleaf Japanese maple has airy, delicate foliage that contrasts with heavy pot, casts interesting shadow. Most maples are commonly propagated from seed.

Mission olive grown from a cutting taken in 1946 and rooted in damp sand. Cutting was actually decayed stump you can see in the center of the tree.

Japanese pear, propagated by grafting (see page 24). The tree is 30 years old and as many inches high, has white blossoms and bears edible fruit each spring.

Colorado blue spruce was an unkempt, scrubby looking plant when found in a nursery can. Heavy pruning revealed its structure and opened the branches.

Evergreen trees, bonsai containers in all shapes and sizes. From left to right: Lebanon cedar, lodgepole pine, Japanese pine, variegated juniper, Indian cedar, Himalayan pine, Japanese pine. All but juniper were from seedlings.

Young seedlings make good bonsai. Mexican piñon (foreground), Scotch pine (left), and Japanese black pine were transferred from field to containers.

The layer should be a couple of inches deep, to permit early root development, and the soil should have a good proportion of sharp sand for drainage.

Make furrows about $\frac{1}{4}$ inch deep, or prick holes same depth, and put in the seeds about 3 inches apart, firming the soil back over them. Water with a fine spray that won't wash the soil away.

Keep the flat in a place that gets morning sun, but not strong afternoon sun since this will dry the soil too much and too fast. Keep the soil watered, and pluck out any weeds that get started.

Waiting for seeds to sprout can be like waiting for a pot to boil. The time seems interminable, but one day a little spot of green will appear, and soon it will develop into a pair of leaves, and before long, a few inches of seedling will be stretching above the soil.

Hard-shelled seeds (such as apricot, peach, almond) should be soaked in water overnight before being planted. Such seeds can even be started in water indoors.

Train a seedling

Seedlings you have raised should stay in the flat for a year. Keep an eye out for pests, such as slugs, snails, and earwigs, who thrive on tender leaves.

At the end of a year, cut and lift the seedlings out of the flat with a knife, much as you would slice out portions of a cake. Trim the roots back by about a third, without knocking off all the soil. Pot the seedling in an ordinary clay pot, or even a very small bonsai container if you want to enjoy it in its adolescence, adding fresh soil below and around the root ball.

Once the seedling is in a container, you can start its training as a bonsai. Prune the branches and wire them, if needed, as discussed in the chapter titled "As the Twig Is Bent."

These miniature, or *mame* (pronounce it mommy), bonsai can be kept in tiny pots, for up to five years, or until the plant starts to visually overpower the container. About this time, the seedling should be put into a regular bonsai container.

If you don't care to enjoy the seedlings as *mame* bonsai, plant them right in the ground in a corner of the garden, or some such place where they'll receive good watering and won't be stepped on. If you plant more than one, keep about two feet of space between them, to allow for root growth. Keeping seedlings in the ground for a year or two allows them to grow faster. While in the ground, they can be branch pruned and wired.

In the spring, before the buds have opened, you can take them up, as you would a tree collected in the wild, prune the roots, and pot them.

Cuttings Are Easy

With the exception of pines, almost all plants take to propagation by cuttings. Olive, willows, cotoneaster, firethorn, azaleas, rhododendrons, and boxwood are especially easy to handle and grow well. Starting bonsai from cuttings is faster than starting them from seed.

Cuttings are best made in early spring and fall, just before buds open, or after the new growth has hardened. Since this method of propagation utilizes a section of the parent plant, you can be almost certain that a cutting will reproduce the exact form and quality of the original.

The best cuttings are made from nonflowering sideshoots of vigorous, healthy plants. If the stem snaps, it's ready for cutting. If it bends or crushes, it's too young or too old.

Allow for a cutting 2-4 inches long. With a sharp knife make a clean cut, slanting at a 45 degree angle, about ¼ inch below a node (joint in the stem). Trim the lower leaves from the cutting, but retain the top two or three leaves to provide food for the cutting until roots have formed.

Certain types of coniferous evergreens do better if they are rooted from cuttings with a heel. This means that when you take the cutting you also include a small portion (heel) of the older or larger branch.

Remove a heel cutting from the parent with a sharp knife, being careful not to rip the bark. Trim the heel so that the edges and surface of the cut are smooth.

Some species may be rooted in water, but most cuttings require sand or other media. A flat or a box at least 3 inches deep should be filled to within a half-inch of the top with clean builder's sand. (Don't use beach sand, since it contains salt.) Soak the sand, then make rows 2 inches apart and about an inch deep, or else poke holes into the sand, spaced the same distance.

Dip the end of each cutting in water, then in a hormone-fungicide powder, following the directions on the label. Set the cuttings in the sand, with two or three nodes below the surface, and carefully firm sand around the stem.

Keep the medium damp, but don't allow it to be-

Softwood cuttings promise more success to beginner, because they root more readily than hardwood. Under glass some softwood cuttings may root within 3 weeks.

Heel cuttings are often taken from semi-hardwood plant material: arborvitae, azalea, cotoneaster, daphne, jasmine, lilac, myrtle, pyracantha, weigela, yew.

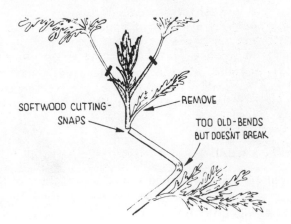

SOFTWOOD CUTTING-SNAPS

REMOVE

TOO OLD-BENDS BUT DOESN'T BREAK

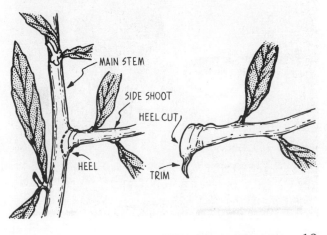

MAIN STEM

SIDE SHOOT

HEEL CUT

HEEL

TRIM

Coast live oak *(Quercus agrifolia)* is good example of a multi-trunked bonsai. In ground this California native may grow to 70 feet and have a trunk six feet in diameter. The specimen shown above is 10 years old, was potted from a nursery can.

Important step in making a cutting is stripping off lower leaves (first step illustrated on page 11). Make hole in soil, insert cutting, firm soil, water.

Glass jar inverted in pot makes a good propagating case for cutting. Raise jar occasionally to admit fresh air and to keep mold from forming.

come waterlogged or the cuttings will rot. Shade the cuttings for several days.

Well rooted cuttings should be treated as seedlings (see pages 18 and 19). Keep them in the rooting medium for at least a year, then in the autumn transfer them to a pot, after root trimming, or plant them in the ground for faster growth.

A Whole Tree by Layering

Layering is a simple and convenient method of increasing a plant by rooting branches while they are still attached to the parent plant. Maples, azaleas, cryptomeria, pomegranate, and many others lend themselves to this method of propagation, which is best carried out in mid-spring. Through layering you can obtain a bonsai that is on its way to being a tree with a well established form and branch structure. The root system of layered plants is not at all troublesome since you have no taproot to contend with.

From Balled Tree to Bonsai

If you come across a balled tree even three or four feet tall and see it as a potential bonsai, buy it — it may not be there next time.

When you get it home don't cut it down to size all at once. Pot it in a big container, one large enough that the root ball will not be disturbed. (Plant the entire root ball; the burlap will rot.) Be sure to leave about 1½ inches between the top of the soil and the edge of the container for good watering. Cut off the top third of the tree, prune the branches to shape, and wire, if desired.

Leave the giant bonsai in the container for two years, continuing to prune and shape it. Then transplant it to a smaller container, cutting back the roots to fit. Shape for another year, then go to a smaller container, and so on until the tree is the size you want.

Earth layering

With a plant that is growing in the ground, either in your garden or in the wild, choose a branch with some personality, one long enough to reach the ground. Bend it down, make a slit underneath, and insert a pebble to hold it open. Hold the layered stem in place and surround it with soil to which has been mixed some sand and peat moss. Support the upright shoot with a stake. The process is illustrated at the foot of this page.

Softwood plants will root in 6-8 weeks. Once they are rooted, sever them from the parent plant and pot them or else plant them out in prepared soil. Keep new buds pinched off until the layered stem develops a good root system.

With rhododendrons, azaleas, and certain other hardwood shrubs, old branches are best layered. If the layered area is kept moist, most layers will root within a year and can then be severed from the parent plant and potted or planted.

Air layering

Air layering produces quick results and there is little risk to the parent plant. It's especially useful if you have a plant growing in the ground that has outlived its usefulness as a decorative shrub or garden plant, or a plant that has good top growth but a scrawny or misshapen base.

All you need is some polyethylene sheeting, a little string, some sphagnum moss, a sharp knife, and a bit of luck. In late spring, after frost danger is past, select a branch or the top of the main trunk with a diameter of a pencil up to an inch. If you choose the

Almost any of the supple branches on this variegated pittosporum could be layered by bending it down to the earth. The process is described on this page.

Earth layering. Select a flexible branch close to the ground. Mark a point about 12 inches from end of the branch, just below a node. Make hole in ground about 4 inches deep. Mix soil with equal parts of peat moss of ground bark and sand.

On underside of branch make a slanting cut. Bend branch back slightly, being careful not to crack it, and insert pebble in cut. Bend branch into hole and anchor with wire loop. Stake end of branch into vertical position. Add prepared soil, then water.

Woody plants should be ready for transfer to bonsai container in 9 months to a year. Check to see if layer has rooted by removing some soil on top. If you see roots, sever the stem just below the original cut, retain some of the original soil, and pot.

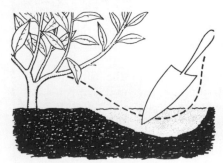
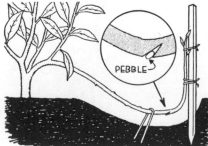

🌳 Bonsai by Air Layering

AIR LAYERING is a sure-fire way to obtain a bonsai with a pre-established form. Choose a garden shrub or a plant in the wild with handsome (and healthy) top growth and proceed as explained in the text and illustrated below. Wire the branches either during the waiting period or after the tree is potted.

1. Make the cut.

2. Dust with hormone powder.

3. Wedge a pebble.

4. Surround with sphagnum.

5. Wrap with plastic.

6. Remove when rooted.

7. Plant in a box.

8. Inspect the roots.

9. Repot and prune.

Satsuki azalea, a group often seen in bonsai form, owing to its bright flowers. This plant is about 50 years old. Azalea is propagated by cutting or layering.

Citrus trees are most commonly propagated by grafting. Meyer lemon, shown here, yields good cuttings, produces fragrant flowers and fruit, even in container.

top of a small tree, you'll have the bonsai well on its way to final shape.

Below a node, either make a slanting cut a third through the stem and insert a pebble to keep it spread apart, or remove a ring of bark about ¾ inch wide, scraping all the way down to the heartwood. Dust the cut lightly with hormone powder, wrap the area with a good-sized ball of damp sphagnum, and tie it in polyethylene film, binding it securely above and below the cut with string or wire ties.

In a month or two you should see roots in the sphagnum. Then you can separate the youngster from the parent plant and either set it into a box of soil until it develops further, or pot it directly into a bonsai container. If the layering doesn't "take," the plant won't be harmed. Try again at another location.

Dividing Is Simple

Dividing is propagating by separating the roots of a parent plant. Mid-spring is the best time. Bamboo takes well to this method of propagating, as do wisteria, pomegranate, and daphne. Merely dig out the root mass with a spading fork, cut it apart with a sharp knife to form new sections, and plant them in freshly prepared beds or in training pots with fresh soil. Keep the pots watered, and don't begin top training until the new roots have established themselves (about 6 months).

Before potting divided roots, it is well to dust them with rooting hormone or with sulfur, to prevent rot.

Grafting Is Touchy

Grafting requires considerable patience and a fair amount of practice. It's not always as successful as some of the other methods of propagating, and the results are long in forthcoming. Nevertheless, the process is an interesting one to try, and a successful graft can give you quite a thrill.

Grafting scions should be taken from trees whose leaves are good for bonsai but whose growth is slow, and they should be grafted to trees of the same species that are good growers. For example, the five-needle Japanese white pine (*Pinus parviflora*) is often grafted to the Japanese black pine (*Pinus thunbergii*). The former has small, handsome needles; the latter is a faster grower.

The greatest drawback to grafting bonsai is that even after a graft has successfully taken, an ugly scar remains. The best answer is to make a graft as low as possible in the hope that it can later be hidden in the planting behind a rock or grasses.

Grafting is usually done in the winter or early spring, when the buds are dormant and just as the sap begins to flow. There are many methods of grafting, but the easiest for bonsai work are cleft and whip grafting.

In making a top cleft graft (see drawings this page), cut the stock across squarely at a point where it is ¼ to ½ inch thick. Lay a grafting tool or a sharp knife across the end of the cut and tap it in with a small hammer to make a cleft about ½ inch deep through bark and all. Knife-cut the scion to fit the cleft, and insert it, making sure that the cambium layers (the soft layer of tissue between the bark and the wood) match. Leave a little of the cut surface of the scion exposed above the surface of the stock, since this makes for a stronger union. Finally, cover the cut surfaces with grafting wax.

Keep grafted plants out of the direct sun, and water them well for two weeks. After about six months, the scion should show some indication of sprouting or growing. If it shows no life after eight months, forget it and the following spring start all over again, or try some other method of propagating.

Whip grafting allows you to graft small scions on small stocks. It's a handy method for adding a branch to a tree in a place that has an unsightly gap that can't be filled by wiring or tying another branch into place. Make a slanting cut through both stock and scion. Then make a second cut into each, starting about a third of the distance from opposite tips, cutting almost parallel to the original cut. Fit the scion and stock together, wrap or tape them lightly, and cover the union with grafting wax.

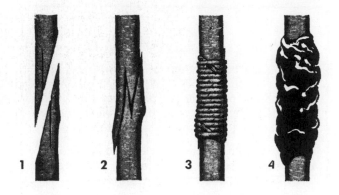

Whip graft. (1) Make slanting cuts through stock and scion, then second cut through each. (2) Fit together. (3) Wrap or tape tightly. (4) Cover with wax.

Cleft graft. Split the end of a square-cut stock and slip in pre-trimmed scions, matching cambium layers of stock and scion. Cover cuts with grafting wax.

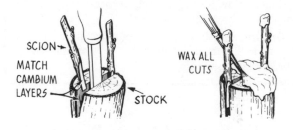

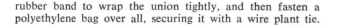

Cleft graft on pine. Short scion (terminal bud with about an inch of stem) should fit snugly into cleft cut in stock. Use

rubber band to wrap the union tightly, and then fasten a polyethylene bag over all, securing it with a wire plant tie.

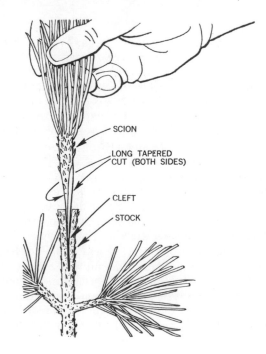

SCION
LONG TAPERED CUT (BOTH SIDES)
CLEFT
STOCK

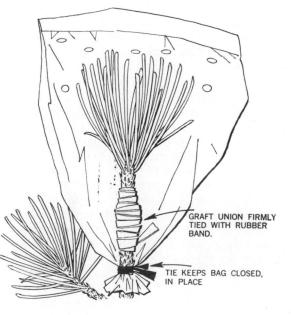

GRAFT UNION FIRMLY TIED WITH RUBBER BAND.

TIE KEEPS BAG CLOSED, IN PLACE

Propagating...Which and How

What is the best method of propagating? It all depends on the species — and on personal preference. Some plants can be propagated by several methods, others by only one. Following is a general guide to the more common bonsai species.

Seed: Maple, beech, pomegranate, ginkgo, zelkova, tupelo (sourgum), liquidambar (sweetgum), larch, buckeye, sweet chestnut, spruce, pine.

Seedling: Birch, beech, zelkova, peach, pomegranate, hornbeam, hawthorn, flowering quince, flowering crabapple, fir, pine, bald cypress, yew, larch.

Cutting: Azalea, rhododendron, olive, daphne, willow, poplar, wisteria, flowering quince, forsythia, tamarisk, coast redwood, bald cypress, spruce.

Layering: Wisteria, maple, camellia, azalea, zelkova, pomegranate, flowering quince, forsythia, willow, crape myrtle, cryptomeria, Yeddo spruce.

Grafting: Wisteria, ginkgo, pomegranate, flowering apricot, plum, peach, pear, persimmon, crabapple, cherry, maple.

Importing Mature Plants

Bonsai can be imported from Japan, but they must undergo severe fumigation before they can be allowed to enter this country. It can be a great disappointment to buy a tree in Japan, then have it perish through not being able to survive the agriculture inspection and quarantine. The picture isn't all black, however, since many trees are brought in and most do manage to live through the treatment.

The best time to import trees is during their dormant period. They are less likely to be harmed by fumigation. If a plant comes in by air (the most expensive way of shipping a bonsai) or as ship's cargo, have a customs broker clear it and bring it to the agriculture building at the port of entry. Only a broker can handle such a plant until it has been cleared. If a tree is brought in on a ship as passenger's baggage, it will first have to be cleared by customs, along with other baggage. Then a member of the ship's personnel must take it to the agriculture building, and the owner may collect it after fumigation. In either case, proof of ownership (customs declaration) is necessary before you can pick up the tree.

When a tree is prepared for export shipment, all the soil is washed from its roots, and the roots are

Flowering quince in bloom several weeks after potting (photos on page 46). Quince can also be propagated from seedlings, from cuttings, and by layering.

wrapped in damp sphagnum moss. When the plant arrives, it is placed in a type of gas chamber and exposed to methyl bromide to eliminate diseases and parasites. The gas upsets the moisture balance of a tree and tends to dry it out. This is perhaps the greatest danger affecting the survival of imported trees.

As soon as your tree is released to you, get it home and keep it out of light and drafts. To prevent further drying out, spray both the foliage and the root ball with water. Don't attempt to repot the tree immediately, because exposing the roots will cause them to dry out much faster. Wait about 24 hours, spraying the foliage as often as possible in this time, then repot as you would a nursery tree.

If you plan a bonsai-buying trip to Japan, be sure to check with the Plant Quarantine Section of the United States Department of Agriculture to find out which trees cannot be imported and which trees have a poor survival rate on importation. The USDA will also be helpful in giving you further information on customs regulations and shipping.

No self-respecting practitioner of the arts would be caught creating a precise duplicate of a natural object. But the greatest test of the bonsai artist is how true to natural forms he can make his subjects. Trunk, foliage, and roots are the elements of reality. The myriad combinations of these elements can be fairly classed into five bonsai styles that are a reasonable guide to the enthusiast striving to capture that elusive essence.

No plant is too unusual for the bonsai enthusiast. This tree is creeping fig *(Ficus pumila),* normally a climbing vine.

The Art of Imitation

A PAINTER WHO ATTEMPTS to reproduce exactly a scene from nature is called a realist. A musician who tries to imitate perfectly nature's sounds is called a nonidealist. A bonsai fancier who duplicates natural forms is called an artist.

Many of the arts frown on copying, using the materials of that art. If a duplicate visual impression is desired, a camera usually does a better job than paints or pencils. If a copy of a sound is wanted, a tape recorder is the answer rather than woodwinds or brasses. But in bonsai, a near-perfect reproduction of one natural form with another natural form is the ideal. This is one area where deception is encouraged. Indeed, deception becomes truth, for a true bonsai is a plant that reproduces the many characteristics that make up a mature tree.

Artificially distorted trees, such as those with trunk or branches tied in knots or those trimmed in the shape of animals, are in no way related to bonsai. Bonsai copies, but it copies natural forms.

Bonsai are intended to be a replication of nature and so must follow nature's ways. This is not to say, however, that a particular species chosen for bonsai must always be trained in only the same growth habit of the mature tree of that species. Star jasmine is a low-growing shrub or a vine. When used for bonsai material, star jasmine can be trained to resemble a twisted upright tree (see the photo on page 8). The point to be noted is that although a plant may duplicate a mature plant of either its own species or of another species, an artificial form is never given.

There are potted plants, and there are potted plants. A bonsai is not just another potted plant. Although its training and needs are specialized, they are simple and require little effort. Since a bonsai is either a tree or a plant made to imitate a tree, all of the elements of its makeup must be directed toward carrying the illusion to its fulfillment. There are three basic elements of any plant that contribute to its potential as bonsai material: the trunk, the foliage (branches and leaves), and the roots.

The Trunk Tells the Truth

The trunk is perhaps the most important element of a bonsai. It tells more about the age of a plant than any other. Whatever the true age of the bonsai itself, if the trunk does not indicate maturity the illusion is not complete. Little can be done to make a tree look old if the trunk does not establish age to begin with.

Generally, the greater the girth of the trunk, the older the tree. Thick trunks can be carried to an extreme, however. There are bonsai less than a foot in height with a trunk 3 inches in diameter. Such a trunk is wondrous, but when considered in regard to the scale and balance of the entire tree, it is grotesque and entirely out of proportion.

A trunk should taper gradually toward the top of the tree. If a trunk is too short for good balance, train one or two main branches to extend its line and so give the appearance of a longer trunk that is more in balance. A trunk that's too long shouldn't be chopped off squarely. Instead, cut it at an angle at a point where a good-sized branch joins it. Then pare the cut with a sharp knife to blend trunk line into branch line. The cut will heal and the trunk will seem to have changed direction abruptly, owing to a natural cause.

The ruggedness of a trunk should be allowed to develop naturally. Never try to make a trunk look old or weather-beaten by gouging it with a knife or intentionally bruising it. If a branch or stub must be cut from the main trunk, try to cut it as close to its point of attachment as possible. Trim the cut flush with the trunk, then carve out a slight depression with a sharp knife. The wound will heal and the scar will be flush and barely discernible.

Bonsai purists frown on using tools at all to prune or cut away undesirable wood. Instead they attempt to twist or splinter off branches so they will appear broken by natural forces of wind or lightning. The practice is effective when successful, but wrenching at branches with abandon can damage a tree badly.

There is a variety of levers, jacks, and clamps that can be used to straighten a crooked trunk or put a bend in a straight one. Such medieval torture devices are fearfully complex and their misuse can harm a plant. Unless the trunk of a tree can be bent with the aid of heavy wire, it is better left as is.

Foliage—Reflector of Seasonal Change

The ideal bonsai would be one on which flowers, fruits, and foliage were tiny and in perfect scale with the size of the tree. Unfortunately, not all plants grow this way when they are cultivated as miniatures. There may be some decrease in leaf size from that of a normally grown tree of the same species, but complete miniaturization is not perfect and with many plants it is insignificant.

This is why certain plants simply do not make good bonsai material. In spite of many desirable characteristics, leaves remain at full size and so are all out of proportion. A good example is the tulip tree (*Liriodendron tulipifera*). This is a plant that grows well in a container. It has a heavy, rugged trunk with deeply wrinkled bark. It has a good root structure. Its leaves are of an unusual and striking shape. However, the leaves obstinately remain at their normal size — some 4 inches across — which offsets the effect of any bonsai training.

Plants used for bonsai should have small leaves, or at least leaves that are not large. The avocado is an easily propagated plant, but its leaves are too big. The zelkova (*Z. serrata*), on the other hand, has tiny elm-like leaves, which is one reason it's a favorite of bonsai fanciers. Pomegranate, certain maples, some oaks, and most species of pine and spruce have small leaves, or needles, and so make good bonsai.

Many deciduous bonsai provide a great deal more visual enjoyment than evergreens since they offer constant change with the seasons. In the spring, the buds open and tender new leaves appear. Throughout the summer, the full foliage holds the tree to its characteristic form. In the autumn, the color changes make a different plant out of the same bonsai. Then through the winter, an entirely new form is created by bare branches.

Main branches should rise strongly from the trunk. There should be no weak twigs straggling out to the sides. The trunk should dominate and give the tree its basic form. Portions of trunk and branches should show through the foliage in places.

Roots—Transition from the Earth

Aside from their important role of drawing nourishment from the soil, the roots of a bonsai also play an important part in establishing the character of a tree. An exposed root structure does a great deal in lending age to a tree, especially if the roots that show are of good girth and form.

A bonsai need not have an equally developed root system on all sides of the base. One-sided systems can be trained over a rock, which will then support the weak side of the tree. Twisted and tangled roots are

Gnarled trunk of this Western juniper is evidence of great age. Note scaly bark, the ragged stump, the extreme girth. Tree is more than 100 years old.

Foliage differences are great even between conifers. Shorter needles of shore pine (right) are in better proportion for bonsai than those of black pine (left).

Roots of this tree were for many years covered with soil, but in repotting were left exposed (the plant was potted higher) because of their character.

not desirable and should be straightened out before potting or repotting a tree.

Seedlings develop good root systems sooner than cuttings. Trees collected in the wild and nursery plants very often have good looking roots, which can be exposed to an advantage when the plant is put into a container to begin life as a bonsai.

Front and Back of a Tree

Just as many people claim to have a best profile, a bonsai has an aspect that is the best for viewing. The planting and all shaping are done with the front of the tree in mind. A tree is always displayed — either singly or with other trees — with its front to the front. When bonsai are displayed at shows one of the most important points of judging is the front of a tree.

Before transferring a plant from a nursery can to a container and starting its training as a bonsai, be sure to establish the front of the tree. When you start a seedling or a cutting on the road to becoming a bonsai, always train it with the front in mind. In considering a tree in the wild, inspect it on all sides to determine the front. A plant that does not have a real front will seldom make a good bonsai.

The front should show a good view of the main trunk. Often the largest part of the trunk should be seen. The main trunk must be clearly visible from the base to the first branch, and it must also show for a good portion of the height of the tree. The upper portion of the trunk should have a slight forward lean.

Heavy foliage or clusters of fruit or blossoms are not necessarily front-determining characters. Everywhere on the tree, but most especially from the front, there must be a good balance among branches and a good relationship between branches and container. No part of a branch should extend across the trunk.

Dimension is given a tree by its branches. A bonsai should not look flat, like an espaliered plant. Also, a tree should not appear lopsided or top heavy because of a bad distribution of fruits or flowers. Remember that leaves and blossoms are going to change with the seasons. The trunk and the main branches don't change, therefore they are more important for establishing the basic form of a tree.

If all this is the front, what is the rear of a bonsai? The rear should be everything the front is, but to a lesser degree. Although the greatest emphasis is given to the front, the rear should not be neglected nor should it be chopped off flat. From the rear there should also be a view of much of the trunk, and the appearance should be one of good dimension and balance. There should be a harmonious arrangement of branches, with no unsightly gaps. By looking down on a bonsai you can often spot flaws.

🌳 Growth Habits of Some Bonsai Material

THE PLANTS LISTED here and on the facing page are most often trained in the bonsai styles indicated. Note that some trees appear under several groups, indicating that there is more than one way to shape a branch.

This listing, along with the seasonal care chart on pages 78 and 79, plus the suggested plants given occasionally, should serve as a guide to bonsai species. Use the silhouettes as reminders of general tree shapes.

PLANTING

One tree

Cedar	Cryptomeria	Spruce	Zelkova
Fir	Cypress	Larch	Maple
Juniper	Hemlock	Elm	Flowering trees
Redwoods	Pine	Oak	Fruiting trees

Several trees

Cedar	Fir	Birch	Maple
Spruce	Juniper	Beech	Elm
Redwoods	Alder	Oak	Zelkova
Hemlock	Ash	Ginkgo	Sweetgum

TRUNK

Single trunk

Redwoods	Fir	Zelkova	Firethorn
Yew	Cryptomeria	Ginkgo	Azalea
Pine	Beech	Cedar	Maple
Spruce	Alder	Elm	Ash

Multiple trunk

Juniper	Azalea	Firethorn	Ivy
Vine maple	Oak	Beech	Ginkgo
Ornamental figs	Olive	Pomegranate	Fruiting trees
Holly	Birch	Dogwood	Flowering trees

ATTITUDE

Upright

Pine	Redwoods	Maple	Ginkgo
Fir	Spruce	Elm	Birch
Cedar	Hinoki cypress	Bamboo	Ash
Hemlock	Larch	Zelkova	Beech

ATTITUDE (Continued)

Slanted

Juniper	Maple	Beech	Ash
Pine	Azalea	Birch	Hawthorn
Spruce	Pomegranate	Olive	Fruiting trees
Oak	Star jasmine	Larch	Flowering trees

Cascaded

Pine	Honeysuckle	Firethorn	Fig
Atlas cedar	Azalea	Maple	Wisteria
Sargent juniper	Chrysanthemum	Olive	Cotoneaster
Jasmine	Camellia	Hawthorn	Flowering trees

FORM

Straight

Cryptomeria	Fir	Ginkgo	Ash
Cypress	Yew	Elm	Birch
Cedar	Spruce	Zelkova	Beech
Pine	Redwoods	Maple	Willow

Twisted

Juniper	Olive	Beech	Azalea
Pine	Spruce	Apple	Oak
Cypress	Flowering apricot	Wisteria	Maple
Firethorn	Quince	Holly	Pomegranate

BASE

Earth

Spruce	Redwoods	Zelkova	Olive
Cedar	Pine	Elm	Birch
Juniper	Maple	Ginkgo	Azalea
Hemlock	Star jasmine	Wisteria	Fruiting trees

Rock

Spruce	Yew	Larch	Pomegranate
Cypress	Pine	Beech	Firethorn
Hemlock	Maple	Ash	Crabapple
Juniper	Azalea	Cotoneaster	Oak

Exposed root

Juniper	Hemlock	Maple	Fig
Yew	Cypress	Olive	Beech
Spruce	Tamarisk	Ginkgo	Wisteria
Fir	Pine	Larch	Pomegranate

Strawberry guava, 100 years old, trained in slanted style. Tree has multiple trunk that is twisted and contorted. Base of tree is earth, with exposed roots.

Moss falsecypress (*Chamaecyparis pisifera squarrosa*) planted as single tree with upright orientation. With thinning this variety plants well in a group.

A Flexible Classification

The classification of tree forms, if allowed to get out of hand, can become a ruling discipline. Granted that mature trees have certain basic forms and growth habits, defining the enormous number of styles, shapes, forms, orientations, arrangements, and systems that are possible usually results in total confusion.

There is little merit in breaking the style or habit of bonsai into groups and subgroups unless you are deadly serious about making a lifetime study of the art. To avoid cubbyholes of categories, we have used five basic classes of form. These are named merely for convenience in referring to the habits of a tree.

Planting. Is the bonsai made from one tree, or several trees?

Trunk. Is the trunk single, or multiple?

Attitude. Does the tree stand upright, does it slant, or does it cascade?

Form. Is the trunk straight or twisted?

Base. Does the tree sit directly in the earth, is it growing on a rock, or are the roots freely exposed?

These five general styles can be applied to any mature tree, and hence to any bonsai. Try to keep them and their variations in mind whenever you look at a tree. When you classify a mature tree it helps to determine the style a bonsai should be to duplicate that tree.

Planting—one tree or several

An individual planting is a tree that stands alone because of the mature tree's normal growth habit or because of some special feature of the tree that would be lost in a bonsai group planting. A single tree can stand upright (simulating the growth habits of coast redwood, elm) or it can lean at various angles (as would a normally upright tree under the influence of prevailing winds). Its form can be straight (larch, buckeye) or twisted (oak, apple). A single tree can be grown with its roots deep in the earth, as would a mature tree living in a meadow; with its roots in a rock, as many alpine trees grow; or with its roots exposed, as would a tree with the earth washed away from its base.

In a group planting, the emphasis is not on any one tree but on the group as a unit and its ability to simulate a natural grove or forest. Grouped trees can be upright (as in natural groves of coast redwoods), or they can lean as if they were all exposed to constant wind from one direction. Grouped trees usually have a single trunk, and their form can be straight or twisted, depending on the type of plant and the natural tree that is to be simulated. For example, elms usually have a straight, upright form; grouped pines can have either a straight or twisted form.

Grove of 15 alpine firs in good balance with their flat rock container. Note the variation in size of trees.

Individual Trees. One of the best reasons for not trying to adhere to any set of rules in bonsai, especially in defining growth styles and habits, is that mature trees have widely varying growth habits, depending on their environment. So-called normal growth is determined by conditions that prevail during the life of the tree, and any one species of tree can have several so-called normal growth habits. When the western hemlock grows in an alpine meadow, it is a tall, vertical, straight-trunked tree. At timberline, where it's under the influence of snows, winds, and grows in rocky ground, it may have a multi-trunk form, perhaps grow close to the ground, or even cascade down a rock face.

This is why plants listed below and on pages 30, 31 under certain growth habits may fit into more than one category. Some plants look equally well in either single or group plantings. Most maples and pines can be planted and trained as individual trees, or several of the same species can be trained in one container to give the impression of a clumped group or a scattered grove.

The plants that are best grown as single bonsai usually have some special feature. Most fruiting or flowering trees should be planted singly rather than in groups, since their greatest feature — fruits or flowers — deserves the greatest attention. If such materials were potted in groups, the planting itself would detract from this important feature. A few such plants are azalea, flowering crabapple, flowering quince, star jasmine, firethorn, plum, wisteria, sand pear.

There are other characteristic features that make certain species better as individual plantings. Older cork oaks and Sargent junipers often have such coarse, tortured trunks that a single planting is necessary in order that the trunk will be shown to its fullest advantage. The fantastically twisted trunks of very old Sargent junipers would be lost if two or more trees were planted together.

Single, upright trees are the easiest to train. Usually all you have to do is set the tree in a container (see the chapter on care). Often, little wiring is necessary.

If an upright plant from nursery stock is to be modified to a slanted or cascaded attitude, tilt the root ball before planting. You'll have to brace or wire the tree for support or tie down the root ball until the roots have established themselves in the soil.

Cascaded bonsai (as made with Deodar cedar, certain pines, willows) should be planted as single trees. A clump of several stems detracts from the unity of a cascade.

A Grove of Trees. Straight, upright trees, such as elm, liquidambar, and maple, look well as single trees. These same trees are sometimes even more effective planted in groups. Beech and birch in their natural state grow in groves, and look good planted this way for bonsai. Trees of a group planting may be all upright (this is the most common way of planting zelkova), they can lean (common with pine and spruce), they can be scattered randomly (beech grows this way in nature), or several trees can be clumped together (birch and spruce grow this way in the wild).

Usually trees of the same species are grouped, but two different species (seldom more than two) can also be planted in one container. A few evergreens may be planted together with several deciduous trees for a charming effect. If you combine more than one species, don't mix the trees, but keep groups of each

Naturally slanted form of trunk of this conifer was hidden by heavy foliage and deep nursery can. Pruning exposed the style tree should take.

Multiple trunks rise straight from a common point, then fork out to give this cherry plum its particular character. Broken trunk adds to mature look.

species together. In keeping with the Japanese ideal of harmony in dissymmetry, always make up a group planting with an odd number of trees, never an even number.

Each tree of a group planting is considered an individual plant. Nevertheless, all the trees are also considered collectively and should be arranged and

---

A Grove from a Single Tree

There is a fairly simple way to create a fine grove of trees, beginning with but a single specimen. To the uninitiated, this is one of the dark secrets of bonsai.

Take a tree with a well developed trunk and with several good-size branches growing somewhat straight out from the trunk. Leaving several main branches along one side, cut off all other branches on the tree, leaving small stumps. Thin the roots.

Now plant the tree *on its side*, with the cut stumps down and the remaining branches up, leaving a little of the trunk exposed above the surface. Flatten the thinned-out root ball into the soil and cover it by heaping more soil over it. (You may have to wire it down to keep it low.) Be sure you don't cover the trunk completely, but press moss (see page 62) up to it in a natural manner. In time each of the former branches will develop into a main trunk thus forming a grove of trees.

Japanese maples and the five-needled pines lend themselves well to this "raft" style of planting.

---

trained to emphasize the unity of the whole. Branches that grow inward toward other trees should be thinned out to prevent crossovers. Each tree must have individual harmony and balance; but, just as important, each tree must contribute to the harmony and balance of the entire group. This is not to say that one huge mass of foliage should be apparent. Some grouped trees should have their heads trained individually (zelkova), whereas others look better with the foliage of all the individual trees blended somewhat (maples).

A good portion of the trunk of each tree should show, since otherwise there would be little to distinguish the individual trees. Some branches and wood also should be visible, to show the growth pattern from the base up the trunk and on out to the leaves.

Seedlings or small individual bonsai may be put together to make a group planting. Conversely, a group planting, after so many years, may be broken up and the plants planted individually.

All the trees of a group planting should be of roughly the same age and size. However, you can create a nice contrast and a special focal point for the entire group if one tree is slightly larger than the others or has a thicker or more picturesque trunk.

Trunk—single or multiple

Single-trunk trees rise from the ground with one stem that generally doesn't fork out until the first branch. In the wild, without the influence of prevailing winds, the Jeffrey pine and ponderosa pine are single-trunk trees. The quaking aspen, a deciduous tree that often grows in company with conifers, also has a single straight trunk.

The growth habits and characteristics of single-trunk trees are the same as those of individual trees. In addition, single-trunk trees can be planted in groves. They can be upright, slanted, or cascaded. The trunk can be either straight or twisted, and the base can be earth, rock, or exposed root.

Single-trunk trees are perhaps the simplest to shape, since the one stem is the ruling element. Most of the emphasis is placed on it, no matter what the general shape of the tree.

In choosing a nursery plant or a gathered plant for a single-trunk style, make sure that the trunk rises from the ground in a fairly unbroken line. It can be twisted or bent, but it should not fork or branch out for at least the first third of the general height of the tree. Small branches or twigs that are low to the base can be trimmed off with no loss. However, if a heavy branch occurs close down near the greatest girth of the main trunk, don't plan the tree for single-trunk style, since removing such a heavy branch, or even a secondary trunk, may weaken the tree or leave a bad scar. Such a tree would be better used as a multiple-trunk subject.

The whitebark pine and the western juniper often have multiple trunks and huge lower branches that rise from the base. The horsechestnut rises from the ground with a single thick trunk, but this quickly divides into two or more heavy stems. This type of growth is characteristic also of many oaks and of cultivated fruit trees. Multiple-trunk trees may have fairly straight trunks (as does the Pacific dogwood), or the trunks may be twisted (as with many oaks and the European olive).

Multiple-trunk trees are best planted as individual bonsai, since their forking habit causes a division of interest.

Many nursery plants — several of them shrubs — with a multiple-trunk habit make fine bonsai. The dwarf mugho pine (*Pinus mugo mughus*) is a short, shrubby conifer with several stems, or with a stubby main stem that branches out close to the earth with several stout secondary trunks. It is best trained with an open, clustered foliage growth rather than as a balled form.

Many species of azalea can be found with multiple trunks, and these often look best with the foliage trained not in separate clusters, but in a unified manner. When the flowers are in bloom they form one solid mass of color.

Multiple-trunk plants are often trimmed high to show the forking habit.

Attitude—upright, slanted, cascaded

In nature some trees are most often seen growing in an upright attitude. Most mature oaks have a spreading branch habit, and their trunks are usually multiple

Slanted, windswept style of this lodgepole pine was way in which the tree was growing when gathered from the wild. In natural habitat, coastal winds often bend young trees low to ground, keep them there into maturity. Height is 12 inches.

and twisted, but their attitude is somewhat upright or vertical. To classify attitude as upright means that, in general, the main trunk line runs in a vertical direction before becoming divided or branching out. Such trees usually are not under the influence of strong winds that would deform them, and so they remain fairly upright for most of their lives even though their branches are twisted and gnarled.

Slanting trees are leaners — trees that are not vertical yet are not cascaded. The so-called windswept style is a slant style — it simulates a tree that has been forced by the wind into nonvertical growth, a tree whose trunk departs from the vertical.

Many gathered trees and many nursery plants are already naturally slanted, and you can retain that orientation when you put them into a container as bonsai. You can make a vertical tree into a slanted style simply by tilting the plant when potting it for bonsai. Of course, it is not enough merely to lean the tree to one side — you must also trim the branches and foliage to be in harmony with the attitude of the tree.

Don't try to make a slanted style out of a vertical style by sticking the trunk in the ground at an angle and letting it go at that. Keep the proper relationship between base, container, trunk, and branches.

A cascaded tree is one that is neither upright nor slanted. To be more specific, it is a tree whose growth habits take the greater part of the foliage *below* the horizontal.

A cascaded style represents a tree in nature that is growing down the face of a steep embankment or a rocky face. It represents a tree that has been forced flat against the earth.

Cascaded trees are trained much in the same manner as are slanted trees, only much more so. This style is perhaps a little more difficult to achieve well, if only because training a tree in this manner takes longer. For your first attempt at trying to train a tree in the cascaded manner, it would be better to begin with a normally low-growing species rather than to use an upright grower and try to form it into a violently unnatural form. Prostrate junipers are especially well adapted to this style. In addition, they are hardy, tolerant of poor soil, compact, are moderate to fast growers, and have a good foliage color variance.

To make a prostrate juniper into a cascaded style, after potting it on a slant, simply trim all the foliage away from the under side and wire or tie down the main trunk. This will serve as a start. As the plant takes to its new life, you can refine your training by selecting the strongest branches to remain and giving them more interesting shapes by wiring.

Some old cascaded plants will grow far below the bottom edge of the container and so must be set on a small stand. This will allow the cascade to hang below the stand without touching it.

Many flowering plants look attractive cascaded. Wisteria, chrysanthemum, star jasmine, and others, appear as a sheet of blossoms when in full flower. This cascaded form is not normal with Deodar cedar, but the tree is striking when cascaded and is flexible enough to be easily trained.

Form—straight or twisted

The dawn redwood is perhaps the best natural example of a straight-form tree. Almost never is a bonsai redwood trained in any other type of growth habit, since its character is in its clean, straight trunk line that carries from the base right on up to the tip.

In selecting a nursery plant for a straight form, make every effort to get the plant with the straightest trunk. Selecting is much simpler than trying to straighten a crooked trunk.

This might be said also for a twisted form style. Rather than starting with a sturdy straight trunk and through clamps, or tying, or wiring, trying to deform it over a long period, you're far better off choosing a tree with a twisted trunk to begin with.

Generally, a twisted form implies great age, since it gives a gnarled, weathered look to the tree. With multiple-trunk trees, trunks may be twined around each other — as is often found with olive and pomegranate. If two or more trunks are to be trained to twine in this manner, make sure the effect is natural looking. Avoid any possibility that the twisting might look man-made.

Unless twisted trunks do definitely intertwine, try to keep them well separated in order that there will be no distracting crossing lines of trunks or primary branches.

Base—earth, rock, or exposed root

Before beginning the actual work of potting a tree for bonsai, always try to have in mind an idea of how the tree will best stand in the container. This will depend to a great extent on all of the factors previously considered. Don't plant a tree one way, then decide it would look better another way and uproot it to make the change.

The earth style of planting is probably the easiest, and the one most likely to ensure survival of the plant. Nevertheless, think of the base of the planting in terms of the overall theme. Upright trees most often are planted in the earth. Slanted and cascaded forms frequently have exposed roots, or are trained on rocks, since they usually represent plants that grow along rock faces or in situations where earth is washed out from around roots. Detailed training information is given in the chapter on care.

You can make a miniature tree grotesque by imposing yourself on it or you can create a striking original form by working along with nature. Judicious use of the pruning shears effects instantaneous changes that are to a tree's benefit. Finer adjustment of form is wrought by wiring and bending. The total complement of tools in the bonsai kit is simple indeed, since it is built chiefly around fingers and hands.

Wiring and bending are typical bonsai training methods. Without such training this pine would be just another tree.

As the Twig is Bent

FOR ANYONE WILLING to do more than pull a plant out of a nursery can and stick it into an oriental looking container, bonsai offers rich bonuses. Such haphazard culture *may* give you a container plant that *may* survive; but if it does survive, it probably will little resemble any kind of a mature tree.

If you would duplicate a mature tree, you must understand the way mature trees grow. To really know trees, look at them first from a distance to see how they rise from the earth and stand in relationship to their surroundings. Walk around them, to learn how the branches come out of the trunk, how the foliage establishes a form unique for each particular tree. Inspect them close up, to find out how trunks are shaped and textured, how leaves form certain foliage patterns.

Finding out for yourself how and why trees grow

as they do is the first reward. There are less pleasant ways you could spend your time.

The next reward is in translating these impressions to the formation of a small plant. Whether you merely prune a plant into the general form of a mature tree and call it a day, or continue to look after its training year after year, you'll experience a degree of pleasure in bringing about proportion and harmony in a nondescript plant. The longer the training of a tree is carried, the longer this pleasure is prolonged.

Finally, a well planned and carefully trained bonsai is a good thing in itself. Like a flower arrangement, it can enhance and unify a corner of a room or a portion of a garden. Unlike a flower arrangement, its beauty is lasting. Moreover, the beauty of a bonsai changes with the seasons — new growth, full foliage, color changes, bare winter branches.

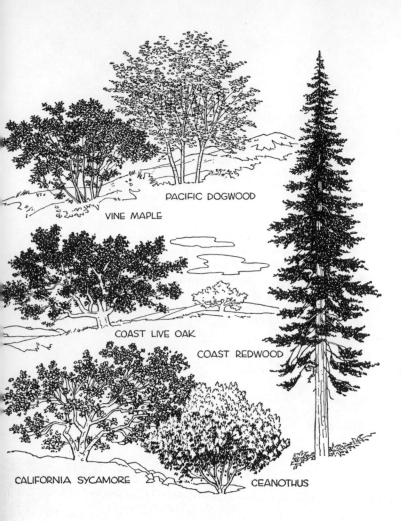

PACIFIC DOGWOOD

VINE MAPLE

COAST LIVE OAK

COAST REDWOOD

CALIFORNIA SYCAMORE

CEANOTHUS

Red alder *(Alnus rubra),* a West Coast native that grows near streams, moist canyons. In natural habitat, this tree grows in much the same twisted manner.

Do you notice trees, or do you *see* them? If you really see them, you'll be familiar with the variety of shapes, orientations, and growth patterns in nature.

The greatest pleasure in bonsai, however, is not in the final product. Even the chances of success or of failure are of relatively minor significance. Your personal satisfaction in doing something you enjoy is the most important.

Working with Nature

There are three principal ways to familiarize yourself with bonsai forms and growth habits. Any one of them will guide you in creating a planting; all three will help you understand the why and how of bonsai.

The way of a tree

The best way to learn about growth habits of trees is to get out and look at trees. Learn to recognize just what makes a tree grow in a particular manner, why a tree is formed in one way or deformed in another.

Trees tend to lean toward water, away from wind, toward lowland. Foliage grows such that it receives the maximum amount of sunlight. Trees that grow in tight groves have most of their foliage high up. Such trees stand straight, and most of the branching reaches up instead of out. Trees that are not crowded together usually have bushy foliage and spreading branches. Some species that receive a great deal of snow are bent close to the ground and have a low spreading habit. Others are tall but have drooping branches.

When you observe trees in the natural state, ask yourself why they grow the way they do. Why do some trees grow in groves? Why do some have straight trunks while others have twisted trunks? Why does a species grow vertically in one place and prostrate in another? How do rocks, soil, wind affect form? Finding answers is fun and valuable to making bonsai look natural and real.

Before touching any plant that you intend to transform into a bonsai — especially a potted nursery tree — study it well. Note the general form of the tree, the angle of the trunk. Pay attention to the branching habit. Try to decide the tree's potential before approaching it with any tools. Once a branch is cut, it can't be replaced.

Cover parts of the foliage with your hands, or carefully move branches in various directions until you can anticipate fairly well the best form the tree will lend itself to as a bonsai. Don't be satisfied with guessing what the plant might look like only after potting and initial trimming, but try to evaluate it for the form and shape it will take in several years.

In this preliminary planning, think of the tree in relationship to a container and to the accessories (such as rocks and moss) that might accompany it. Remember that such accessories are not decorations but parts of the entire planting. They help make the tree look more natural and at home in its surroundings. Don't think of the plant as a dwarfed plant but as a mature tree. This is what you are aiming for — a duplication of nature.

Copying is no crime

You can learn much about raising miniature trees by studying bonsai and talking with the people who have created them. In Japan, bonsai shows and exhibits are well attended events and most of the people who attend the exhibits are novices. In viewing the displayed trees they gain knowledge helpful to their own bonsai problems. Just as important as learning how to do something is learning how *not* to do something. By studying established bonsai you learn what common mistakes have been made and how you can avoid making the same mistakes.

In attending a bonsai exhibition, take along a pad and pencil. Make notes of any striking features or make rough sketches of trees that will be useful in planning your own specimens.

In a few of the larger cities some nurseries specialize in raising and selling bonsai materials, containers, and tools. The owners are invariably helpful and can give you good advice. Their trees are worth studying. Often you'll become acquainted with other novices eager to exchange information.

Another source of information are the numerous bonsai groups and clubs that are especially popular on the West Coast (see page 76 for details). A bonsai group affords good opportunities for meeting other people whose interests may be the same as yours.

Trees shown here are representative of most of the styles discussed in this book. It should be noted that all of these bonsai—as should all bonsai—are not merely container plants, but imitate mature trees growing out in nature.

Five red alders are planted as a grove in a shallow, glazed container. Pruning and periodic nipping keep heavy foliage up and away from the base to show off the strong trunk lines. The coarse bark is a light gray, the branchlets are deep red.

Clubs organize shows and occasionally arrange tours of private collections that might not be seen otherwise.

In attending displays or viewing private collections, pay special attention to imported trees. Many of them are species not available in this country, and so will have a special interest. Other imported species may be available, but you may never see good specimens except at such a showing. Many old trees have been trained by a master in Japan.

Photographs as idea sources

Although photos of bonsai don't always give a precise measure of depth and dimension, they are a valuable source of ideas. Often you'll have a plant you just can't make up your mind about. You won't be able to decide how it can best be trained or what shape of container would be best suited. This is the time when a good collection of photos proves its worth. You can thumb through them and see what others have done with similar trees. You can see what shapes and types of plantings might work for you.

In the homes of real bonsai enthusiasts you'll often see small booklets printed entirely in Japanese and heavily illustrated with photos of valuable trees. The journals give information on Japanese bonsai societies and exhibits and on training. Many persons subscribe to such magazines without being able to read them, but they find the photos very useful. Being published in Japan, the books show trees that are never seen in the United States, many of them classics. (The photos throughout this book show a wide variety of plants and training methods. The captions point out certain features that bear emphasis for each tree. Look at the subjects from other aspects as well. Good trees and faulty ones are depicted in an attempt to present the many forms possible with bonsai material and the numerous ways they can be treated. The photos don't, in every case, represent ideals. There are no totally right or totally wrong ways to handle a particular tree. In many of the illustrations you may see a better way of treating the material.)

Through photographs you can learn what might be done and what not to do. Without becoming a thorough-going critic you can learn to recognize what other approaches could have given the same or better results.

Early Nursery Container Training

The bite of the bonsai bug can become symptomatic in collector's fever. Some enthusiasts have been able to keep a tight rein and stop at two or three trees. Others find they can't stop at all once they've started.

The latter constantly strive for different species or forms.

Once infected, you'll find that you're not only training new bonsai, but that you're also collecting all manner of plants — small and large — and setting them aside for future use. At any moment during a trip to a nursery you may have absolutely no desire to bring home another tree, but then your eye will be taken by some twisted form or some handsome clump of foliage. Soon you realize you have around the garden or against a shaded wall a vast collection of plants in cans, pots, and boxes, all with possibilities as future bonsai.

What do you do with potted plants? Do you just water them when they need it, and hope that someday you'll get around to training them? Or can you develop their potential with a minimum of daily care?

A cluster of miscellaneous plants that receives only water can easily become an annoyance. If not given some attention, they can grow rank and lose all promise as bonsai. They can be weakened or destroyed by disease and pests. They can become a nuisance simply by being in the way.

If you collect a potted plant without expecting to put it into a bonsai container immediately, at least get it started on the road to being a bonsai. Develop the basic form by first pruning the foliage. Try to see, in your mind's eye, the plant in a good container, and shape it by tying or wiring the branches while it's still confined. A year is about the maximum you should keep a tree in a nursery can without root pruning, since many such plants have crowded roots already. If you don't repot or root prune in this time,

---

🌳 **Five Bonsai Planning Questions**

Before laying a hand on a plant that you intend to transform into a bonsai, let your imagination carry you ahead in time. Try to see the tree not as it is now, but as you would like it to be in a year or in several years. Ask yourself the following questions.

1. Is the planting to consist of an individual tree, or is it to be a grove of trees?

2. Is the trunk to be a single stem, or is it to be multiple?

3. Is the best attitude of the tree upright, slanted, or cascaded?

4. Is the general form of the tree straight, or are trunk and branches twisted?

5. Is the base to rise from the earth, grow out of a rock, or expose bare roots?

at least pinch back new growth in the spring or late summer to keep the basic form from getting out of hand.

If it's at all practical, transfer a canned plant to a training pot within a month or so. The pot can be a regular clay flower pot, with a good drain hole in the bottom. If the roots are matted, cut them back by about a third without shaking loose too much soil. Then repot the plant in fresh soil.

Most nursery container plants have a soil level a couple of inches below the rim of the can. In transferring them to a training pot, have the new soil level only about a half-inch down, so you can better observe the trunk and base of your tree. Since you're potting for early training, don't plant moss. This comes later, when the plant is ready to go into its bonsai container.

An initial training period such as this is beneficial since it allows you to make gross corrections or major adjustments without fear of ruining an established form.

Growing Bonsai in the Ground

There is an alternative to having dozens of clay pots and nursery cans sitting around, taking up room alongside the house or garage. It requires a few square feet of well drained ground space that isn't invaded by large tree roots.

Any tree, whether a tiny seedling, a mature collected plant, or a good-sized nursery specimen, can be cultivated right in the ground. Take the plant out of its container, if it's in one, spread the roots a bit without breaking up the soil around them, and set the plant in the ground as you would a young tree. Keep it watered until it takes to its new surroundings. A semi-shaded location is best — preferably one that gets morning sun but not strong afternoon sun.

You can keep plants in the ground for four or five years. They'll usually grow much faster than they would in training pots. Trunks develop a better girth. They can even become a good looking, though temporary, part of the garden.

Don't take such trees up for root pruning. If you plan to leave them in the ground for more than a year, cut completely around each plant every spring with a sharp shovel as you would if you were getting ready to dig it up. This will keep roots from growing far and wide, and will develop new feeder roots close in.

Trees kept in the ground can be grafted and layered. As with other garden plants, give them a good spring feeding.

When you want to transfer such plants to a bonsai container, cut around the roots, as above, a couple of months before, making sure you sever the taproot, if there is one. (Do this in January or February; take

Large pine growing in garden is severely pruned to give "Oriental" effect. This same method of pruning twigs for zigzag appearance is applied to bonsai.

Early branch training of a tree growing in the ground by lashing pieces of bamboo to the branches with cord. Supple branches can be straightened in this way.

Another way to train branches, either on a ground-grown tree or one in container is to tie them in place with wires. Keep a protective pad under the loop.

the tree up in March or April.) Cut around the roots again when you're ready. Take the root ball up and trim it back by about a third, then plant it with new soil in the bonsai container.

This technique works well for most plants and is especially good with azaleas, slow growing pines, maples, elms, and some oaks. Keep an eye on fast growers, such as Monterey pine. If left in the ground for a couple of years, they can get out of hand and you'll have a tree that is just too big to get into a container. Also, be careful with plants that are fussy about their roots. Daphne, persimmon, flowering dogwood, and magnolia are a few such particular plants.

Establishing the Basic Form

Bonsai culture is built around three basic operations: pruning, wiring, and repotting. Some professionals prune and wire before potting. Others pot first, then give the tree a rest for a month or two before working on the foliage. There is no strict order in which these operations must be followed, although pruning before wiring gives a little more working room.

Nipping and pruning don't represent periodic attacks on a tree, as does repotting. A tree usually requires one heavy branch pruning in its life — to establish its basic form. From then on, shaping is done by nipping. The purpose is twofold: to shape and develop the trunk and to control overall size.

Nipping controls new growth

Nipping, or pinching back, is a means of controlling new growth before it becomes woody enough that it must be pruned. By pinching, you can make a twiggy plant more dense. Pinching out all the terminal buds on a branch will force side growth. Instead of one long branch, there'll be several side branches. When you do this all over the plant, the result is overall bushiness.

'Contorta' flowering quince. Biggest plant is 30 years old, small plants are half that age. In Japan, flowering quince are grown in ground for two years to develop a large stem, root-pruned to encourage rooting, then potted as bonsai.

Nipping is easily done with the fingers just as the new growth tips show up. With pines it's sometimes easier to get down into the needles to the new tips with a pair of long tweezers. Be sure to nip needle bearing trees before the "candles" get too long or the new growth hardens.

Undesirable shoots should be nipped in May so other shoots will develop early. Some conifers produce shoots late in the summer as well as in the spring. These also should be kept under control by pinching.

Tiny spurs that appear on the trunk or along heavy branches can be rubbed off with the fingers. If these are left on, they may develop into long, unsightly suckers that will leave a scar when finally removed. Don't try to pinch off hard wood. You may splinter it and cause bad tears in the bark. Instead, use pruners.

Pinch flowering or fruiting trees early in the growing season only. At any other time you might be removing flower buds. Don't pinch jasmine or azalea. Pinching these plants destroys flower buds and will prevent flowering. Instead, prune well just after flowering.

Nipping can be done in a matter of minutes while you're looking at your plants in the morning, just before watering them. Nipping is done not only to shape a plant but also to develop more luxuriant foliage.

The benefits of pruning

Through pruning you maintain plant health by removing dead or injured wood. You control growth and form by getting rid of heavy foliage, crossing branches, suckers, or badly shaped limbs. You keep the plant within the size limits you have imposed on it as a bonsai. You help maintain a balance between foliage and root systems.

The basic points to remember about pruning are these: make your cuts only above a bud, a small side branch, or a main fork. Don't leave too long a stub, or it may become an entry for decay and insects; it's also unsightly. Conversely, don't cut back so far that you cut into main branches or they may be weakened.

If you have a choice of which bud or side branch to cut back to, choose an outside one or one that points in the direction you want to direct new growth. Keep branches growing toward an open space rather than toward each other or the trunk. Crossing branches don't belong in a bonsai.

Do all thinning or shaping by nipping and pruning. *Never shear bonsai.* Shearing a bonsai as you would a hedge gives it a totally artificial form and makes it unrecognizable as an imitation of any living tree. It also encourages too dense foliage and may cause trimmed needles or leaves to brown.

Seedlings need little pruning, but pinch them lightly to direct growth. Gathered trees sometimes need heavy pruning to clear them of extraneous growth or to develop their natural form. Nursery plants need the most attention. Usually they will be overgrown and thick, and they must be opened up to establish the best form.

Before beginning to prune, study the plant from all sides and decide what form you want to end up

Right: Progressive pinching and pruning directs growth into main branches, gives form to what might otherwise be a nondescript shrubby form.

Below: With any plant, pinching out new growth at tips causes forcing of side shoots. To force growth in one direction, pinch tip and all side shoots but one.

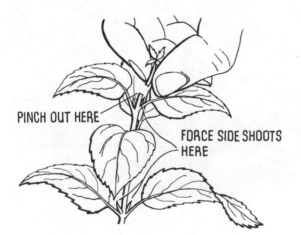

PINCH OUT HERE

FORCE SIDE SHOOTS HERE

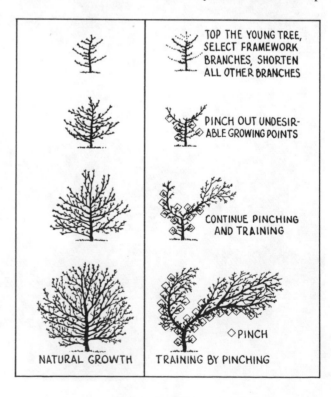

TOP THE YOUNG TREE, SELECT FRAMEWORK BRANCHES, SHORTEN ALL OTHER BRANCHES

PINCH OUT UNDESIRABLE GROWING POINTS

CONTINUE PINCHING AND TRAINING

NATURAL GROWTH

TRAINING BY PINCHING

◇PINCH

with. Never start whacking away at a tree hoping you'll be inspired as you go. Once branches have been cut back severely there is little you can do if you change your mind. However, don't be timid about pruning. The main thing to remember about pruning is when to stop. It's always better to quit just a little before you think you've taken off enough or you'll find "enough" is too much.

How to prune bonsai

With a thick-foliaged tree, first spread the branches so you can see into the center of the plant. Since the trunk establishes the basic form of the tree, you should be able to see it before removing any wood.

Remove all dead, weak, and crossing branches. Then thin the major branches until you've opened the plant and it begins to take on the general form established by the trunk. Remember that each style of tree — upright, slant, multiple trunk, or whatever — requires a different foliage form. If the plant you're working on has been growing in an upright position and you want to alter the style to, say, slanted, don't prune it in an upright attitude, but tip it to about where it should be and work on it from that angle.

Now give attention to the tips of the remaining branches. Cut back new growth, either by pinching or light pruning to short spurs. However, don't take all of it off. Carefully thin out small branchlets, keeping in mind what wood might be wired or tied.

For a regular, somewhat straight form, remove side branchlets and leave the principal center one. Head it back, by pinching or pruning at the end, so it doesn't become over elongated. You can create an irregular zigzag effect (see top photo on page 42) by removing center shoots and most of the side shoots along one side of a fork.

Even if a plant needs heavy pruning, never take off all the foliage. Don't do all of a heavy pruning at one time; do about a third of it first, another third perhaps a month later, and the rest a month or two after that. Except in their dormant season, plants must have a certain amount of leaves in order to manufacture food. If they're all taken off at the wrong time, the plant's nourishment-manufacturing process will be destroyed.

Olive, ginkgo, and certain other species have a tendency to suckering. Long shoots sprout from the base or along branches and grow fast, usually straight up. These should be removed, since they usually spoil the open appearance of a tree. If suckers add to the beauty — which they often do with ginkgo — then leave them.

Sometimes you'll have to remove heavy wood from a thick branch or from the trunk. To avoid a permanent pruning scar, cut the wood as close to the

Where to make your pruning cut: Above promising bud (top left); above promising side branch (top right); at main branch (lower left); at ground (lower right).

trunk as possible. Use a sharp knife to pare the stump flush, then scoop it out slightly with a wood carving tool or chisel. If the wound is larger than $\frac{1}{8}$ inch across, treat it with grafting compound. In time it will heal over and be scarcely visible.

With a group planting, or with a multiple-trunk tree, shorten or eliminate branches that grow inward or cross.

The chart on pages 78 and 79 gives the best seasons for nipping and pruning typical bonsai plants. Although spring and late autumn are usually the best times, most container plants can be pinched back throughout the year, as long as you don't do it too heavily.

🌲 An Accident on Purpose

If you have a pine with a branch or a main trunk that's too long, don't just chop it off. The squared-off stub will never look natural.

Carefully peel the bark away from the end section of wood you want removed. Eventually, that part will wither and die back to where the bark remains. Leave dead wood as an added point of interest. It will eventually turn gray, or you can hasten the discoloration by wiping it with a little household bleach. (Don't get bleach on any living portions.) It will resemble a branch that has been struck by lightning or one broken and torn by wind.

Ready for shaping, a flowering quince as it looked just after being dug from field in December. Note the many crossing branches and the heavy root system.

Here, pruning is nearly finished. Five large branches, several smaller ones, plus twigs, were removed. Spurs kept for blooms. Finished bonsai is shown on page 26.

The Fine Control of Form

Most garden plants are pruned, pinched, and cut back. Many are tied, up, down, or sideways (espaliered). Some are even benefitted by having their roots cut back periodically. The wiring and bending of branches to give form and shape to a plant seems to be unique to bonsai.

Wiring seems more formidable than it actually is. It must be carried out with a little more care than pruning, since it's usually done after a tree has been thinned and the branches that remain are the most important ones. The best way to learn to wire is to try it a couple of times with a larger, fairly limber branch from a garden tree.

Wiring on a large scale

Cut off a few young, tender suckers or shoots from any tree (fruit trees are especially good). They should be about as thick as a lead pencil, and a foot or two long. If they have buds or spurs with leaves, so much the better.

Use regular plastic-or fabric-covered house wire (No. 10 to 20 size). It's common practice to strip insulation off and use just the bare copper wire. Some bonsai men then wrap the bare wire with raffia to keep it from cutting into tender bark. All things considered, it's less trouble to leave the insulation on the wire to begin with.

If you wish to remove insulation from a length of wire it's a simple operation. Straighten the wire and lay it flat on a hard surface, such as a cement floor. Tap the insulation gently with a hammer along the full length of the wire until it splits away, then pull it off.

Take your test branch and wind the wire around it, beginning at the thickest end and working out toward the growing end. Make the turns about ½ inch apart. If you plan to bend the branch to the right (looking down on it), wind in a counterclockwise direction; to bend to the left, wind in a clockwise direction. Avoid wrapping the wire around leaves or buds, and be careful that your hands don't rub any off.

To form the branch, place your thumbs tip-to-tip along the section to be bent. Place your fingers on the opposite side of the branch. Now bend toward you, the thumbs on the inside of the bend. Don't bend too far in one spot, but make a slight bend, then move your hands and bend a little more. Bends that are too sharp can crack the wood or break it entirely.

Practice a few bends with different sizes of branches. To develop a feel for bending, see how far you can deform a branch before it breaks. See if by making slight bends along several inches of a branch you can bend the branch to a right angle. Then make another bend in the other direction to form an "S" shape.

The same general technique is used in bending a living branch on a bonsai. You have to exercise a little more care, since there is less room and there are more damageable twigs and leaves.

What kind of wire

Copper wire is the best. It's flexible, easy to bend, holds bends well, and does not rust. For bonsai work, copper wire is often annealed to make it more flexible, but this isn't really necessary. The Japanese masters anneal by putting their bare wire in a hot fire kindled specifically with rice straw. If you're bent on annealing your wire, you can toss it into the fireplace some evening and fish it out the next day when it's cool. Or you can lay it over glowing charcoal the next time you have a barbecue. (Peel off insulation first or you'll have a fine taste of charred rubber in your chicken or steak.)

You can find odd lengths of leftover wire lying around a house under construction. Or you can buy 10 feet or so of various sizes of "house wire" from a hardware or electrical supply store. The sizes best for bonsai work are Nos. 10, 12, 14, 16, and 18 (the lower the number, the heavier the wire). Number 8 wire is quite heavy and should be used only for a trunk, since it would put too much weight on a branch. Numbers 16 and smaller are light and should be used for very thin branches or for tying rather than bending.

Don't use just one size of wire for all purposes. The size chosen should be such that the wire is more rigid than the branch. Don't use a piece too short for the job, nor one that will be so long it'll be awkward to handle. A wire should be about half again as long as the branch you're going to bend.

Once a branch has taken on its trained form (after a year — see later) you can remove the wire and re-use it. Straighten out the twists and bends, and flatten it by tapping with a mallet.

Wiring is best done during the spring on into early summer, after leaves are out. If you wire too early you may damage unopened buds or tender bark. If you wait until late in the fall, branches become too brittle and may snap with bending.

It's a good idea to let a plant go without water for a day before you plan to wire it. This makes the branches more limber, and they can be bent more easily.

Wiring the branches

Start your wiring and shaping at the lowest point on the tree, whether it be on the trunk or a main branch, and work up to the heaviest branches, then the light branches. Secure the low end of the wire before commencing the winding. At the base of the tree, anchor it by pushing an end deep into the soil. On a branch, begin at the junction with the trunk or at a major fork, and give the end a couple of close turns. If you don't anchor the end of the wire, it'll slip on the branch and scar the bark.

Wind the wire around the branch, keeping the turns about ¼ inch apart. With each turn, hold the previous one tight against the wood. Keep the windings snug but not too tight. If the turns are too loose, the branch won't hold a bend; if they're too tight, the bark may be damaged.

Go carefully around leaves so you don't damage them or their stems, and watch that you don't flatten a leaf tight to a branch. This will take special care with the needle-leaf conifers.

When you reach the end of the wire, or have wired as far as you want to go on a branch, press the end snug against the wood. A stub of wire left sticking out looks unsightly and it can give your hand a bad scratch when you're bending a branch. Use a small pair of wire cutters or nippers rather than pruners to cut wire.

Thick, heavy trunks can be difficult or impossible to bend with wire. It's better to leave them alone, and plan the tree around them. If you're so inclined, you can experiment with one of the thumb-screw torture devices mentioned earlier.

Some helpful considerations in wiring bonsai material. Make sure that the wire is heavy enough to keep a bent branch stabilized in the form you wish to train it.

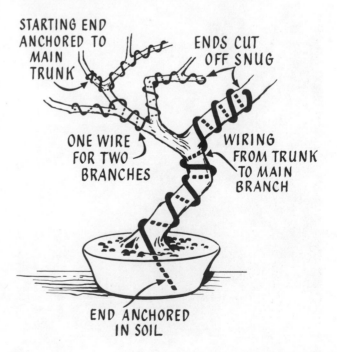

STARTING END ANCHORED TO MAIN TRUNK

ENDS CUT OFF SNUG

ONE WIRE FOR TWO BRANCHES

WIRING FROM TRUNK TO MAIN BRANCH

END ANCHORED IN SOIL

Lodgepole pine pictured on page 37 was started on way to becoming a bonsai in these four stages. First, lower branches were removed to expose the trunk.

Starting at the base of the plant, trunk is encircled with two strands of number 8 wire, which is then divided to single strands at the first main branch.

Trunk and larger branches are gently formed into desired curves. Note that first bend rises gradually from base rather than slanting the trunk sharply.

With wiring and bending completed, tree already has its individuality established, even while still in the can. Next step is transfer to bonsai container.

You can make one length of wire serve for two branches by anchoring the center of the wire at the trunk by a turn or two. Wind one branch with one end, then wind the other with the other end. This method gives good support for both branches.

Shaping by bending

Once a branch is wired properly, the bending is fairly simple. Remember the feel of a wired branch from your practice. Recall how the wood gave as you bent it and how it felt just before it snapped. Be sure to stop any bends before you reach that point.

Keep both thumbs together on the inside of a bend, and hold the branch firmly. It's best not to have a portion of the wire right inside a bend since it has little holding power there. Make bends gradual, and don't attempt any sharp angles or corners.

Again, have in mind what you want to do — the general form you want to create. Once you put a bend in a branch, never try to straighten it or bend it in another direction. This weakens the bark and it may split.

On occasion, no matter how carefully you've wired a branch or how carefully you've formed it, it will snap. Azaleas, sweetgum (*Liquidambar*), and persimmon are notorious in this regard. If the branch doesn't come completely apart, in two separate pieces, there's still hope. Gently bend back the wire *at that point* until the broken ends are joined. Wind some raffia or garden tape around the break and tie it. Then leave it alone. Usually the fracture will heal in a month or two.

If a branch snaps off entirely, there's little you can do except prune back cleanly at the first side branch.

In shaping wired branches, and thus the entire tree, avoid crossing or intermingling branches. You can twist a branch to one side or the other to help fill a gap, but don't distort it in such a way that the result is unnatural. A ragged, sparse tree can often be benefitted by bending branches into open spaces, but if too much wood has been removed in pruning, even wiring can't help.

After you wire a tree, water it and keep it in the shade for a couple of days. Wire should stay on a year to do any good. Take a close look at the tree in about six months to make sure that growth isn't causing the wire to cut into the wood and permanently mark it.

In removing wire, start at the outermost end of a branch and unwind to the anchor end. Here again, watch out that you don't harm leaves, small twigs, or bark. If the wire has been on too long and has started to cut into the branch, don't try to unwind it. Cut it off in small pieces.

Tying and propping

Depending on the tree and its structure, you can hold branches in place by tying instead of wiring. (Sometimes you'll have to do both.) A branch too stiff for bending by wiring can often be bent by tying or propping.

Branches can be tied with thinner wire than that used for wiring. Never knot or twist a tie wire tightly to a branch, but make a very loose loop and protect the wood by slipping a small rubber pad under the wire.

Keep the turns of wire ¼ to ½ inch apart for best results. If leaves are close together along a branch, be careful not to wire over them or over side twigs.

Propping is easy, quick way to separate close-growing trunks or branches. Notch a small "V" in each end of a short stick, then wedge it between trunks.

Combination display shelf, work center for bonsai has a lath overhead to diffuse sunlight and provide frost protection for tender plants. Post construction gives structure airy touch. Four 8-foot 2 by 2's are bolted to 3 by 6's and to 2 by 4's.

Several branches can be pulled downward to give a weeping appearance by running lengths of tie wire from each to the base of the tree. Secure the wires to the trunk, or to exposed roots if there are any. Small weights are also sometimes fastened to limber branches.

If you have a pair of forked trunks or branches that are too close together and there's no place to attach wires to pull them apart, try this: Cut a notch in each end of a stout twig and wedge it between the branches. This will force them apart, and eventually they'll lose their tendency to spring back when the wedge is removed.

A pair of forked branches can be trained closer together by forming a small piece of stiff wire into an "S" shape, then hooking each branch into one of the curves.

In tying or wedging, don't try to force a branch into a new position all at one time. It may split or break. Secure it at about a third or half of full position. A few months later, pull it a little more. This will give the wood time to adapt.

The Basic Tools

Unless you plan to spend many hours with your trees and become deadly serious about it, the basic tools needed for bonsai work are few and inexpensive. You may already have most of them around the house or garden. If not, you can pick them up easily.

Most important is a good pair of sharp pruning shears. The very best, called *masakuni*, are made in Japan. They cost about $8.00. They are especially suited for bonsai work in that they leave a concave depression rather than a flush cut.

Hook-and-blade pruning shears are better than the anvil type for working with bonsai. The former make a clean close cut, whereas the latter leave a little stub and sometimes crush the end of it in the bargain.

In addition to pruners, you should have a garden trowel for mixing soil and for filling containers. You should also have a pair of sturdy cutters or nippers for snipping wire. Have some copper wire in various sizes, as mentioned earlier, and a sprinkling can for watering newly potted specimens. These are the basic tools.

Later, if you find yourself becoming more involved in this most pleasant of hobbies, you may want to add to these basics with a few more simple tools. The following are not absolutely essential, but they do come in handy: Tweezers, for nipping or picking. Brushes, for cleaning and smoothing top soil. Wood carving tool, for cleaning up pruning marks. Hammer and chisel, for splitting rocks. Scissors, for trimming leaves. Knife, for grafting, cutting.

Bonsai Work Centers

For minimum effort at bonsai, you need a minimum of space. At a minimum, have a corner where you can spill dirt and drop cuttings around without having to worry about making a mess. A corner of a porch or patio, even a small outside balcony, works well. You should have good light, since the work gets close at times, but don't work in direct sun. When a plant is out of a container and you're working on the roots they can dry out fast. During warm summer months, a temporary bench set up under a tree will receive good shade and you won't have to be concerned about spilling dirt.

The drawings on this page show some basic work center possibilities (see also the *Sunset* book, *Garden Work Centers*). Any of these can be adapted to bonsai use with little effort. If you plan a permanent work center, you should have a wooden bench about 3 feet high, 6 feet long, and 3 feet wide. This is enough surface to allow you to scatter tools, containers, and plant material freely while working. You can supplement it with shelves for display, or you can display your trees in a separate area, as discussed in the chapter on living with trees.

Under the main workbench you can have bins for soil, and more shelves for storing containers, pots, and rocks. A box or small galvanized can for trash comes in handy. Try to have a water supply handy, to save yourself steps in filling and refilling a container.

A most useful device in a bonsai work center is a turntable or lazy Susan arrangement on top of a small box. This enables you to easily view all sides of a plant without having to lift and turn it. Tools can be kept handy in one place if there's a drawer in the box under the turntable.

Once you become engrossed in working with a plant, you'll be bending, twisting, and craning to see it from every possible angle. Keep a small stool handy, one that will bring your head to the height of the plant.

About Containers

Unlike rocks, moss, or grasses, a container is not actually part of a bonsai scene. Nevertheless, the container must be chosen to complement the tree in

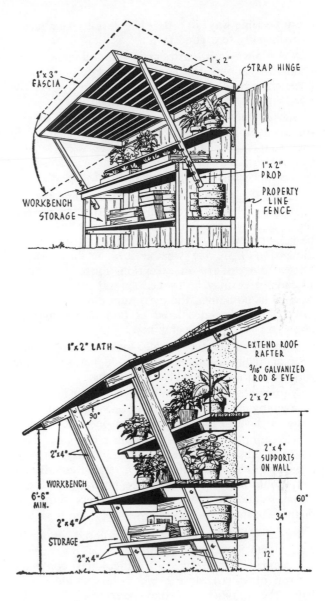

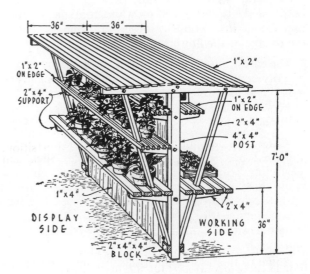

Three multi-purpose garden work centers that work well for bonsai. Unit at top is built against fence, has an adjustable sun shade. Center unit is good in a narrow side yard. The lath overhead is an extension of the house or garage roof. Unit at bottom is a combination free-standing decorative screen, display area, workbench. Display side can face the garden or the living area. Each of these centers can easily be modified to give you another shelf or two.

every possible way in order that it not give a feeling of artificiality to a good tree.

A container must harmonize with and enhance the plant that it holds, in shape, size, and color. None of these characters should be allowed to overpower the tree. First emphasis must always be on it.

Bonsai containers come in five general shapes: round, oval, square, rectangular, and hexagonal. In each shape there is a wide variety of sizes, ranging from an inch across to more than a foot. Each shape comes in a variety of shallowness or deepness.

There is a rule of thumb for determining the size relationship between container and tree. In general, the greatest dimension of the container (whether it be height or width) should not exceed ⅔ the greatest dimension of the tree (whether it be height or width). Cascaded trees are an exception. Since much of a cascaded tree may be trained several feet below the base of its container, the maximum dimension of the plant should be considered as that of the material above the base of the container.

A cascaded planting usually looks best in a round or rectangular container that is higher than wide. The tree should be planted off-center.

An upright style or slanted style is best in an oval or rectangular pot, planted not in the center but about a third of the distance from one end.

A group planting looks best in a rectangular, large oval, or other wide and shallow container. Trees of a group planting shouldn't be arranged equidistant, but should seem as if they were growing randomly. Some should be close together; others should be farther apart.

Be careful about using brightly colored containers, except with flowering or fruiting plants. Pines should be planted in unglazed, earth-colored containers (brown or green), since bright colors would detract from the simplicity of the green tree. Trees that show autumn colors (ginkgo, sweetgum, maple) can be planted in plain green or white containers. Don't use a container whose color is the same as that of the foliage or the flowers.

The safest all-around choice is an unglazed brown or gray container. It has an earthy feel about it and won't detract from any tree. Beware of using containers with ornate decorations or letterings, or those with odd shapes.

Although good containers are costly, lower-priced, unglazed bonsai pots are quite suitable. Slight imperfections can always be turned to the rear. The drain hole in a new container is usually covered with a cemented-in plug. Unless you need a water-tight container for flower arranging, gently tap the plug out with a hammer and a nail, while resting the pot upside-down on a stable surface.

Some of the larger nurseries sell bonsai containers.

Dwarf Tanyosho pine (*Pinus densiflora* 'Umbraculifera') planted in blue, glazed container. This tree develops numerous picturesque cones very young.

If you live in or near a large city that has an Oriental section, you may be able to find them in Chinese or Japanese hardware stores. Stores specializing in imported items usually have a good selection.

Wooden bonsai containers would be cast aside by the purist, but they can enhance a rugged, handsome tree. Use rough redwood, both for its natural appearance and its resistance to rot. Fasten butt joints with dowels to prevent metal stains. The bottoms and feet can be nailed on, since stains underneath won't show.

To bring out the grain on homemade wooden containers, burn the wood with a blowtorch, then remove the charred wood with a wire brush. The container can be darkened with stain. A combination of beeswax, turpentine, and linseed oil rubbed into the outside will give it a dark waxy finish. To prevent rot, treat the inside with a commercial wood preservative (one with a copper base — don't use creosote). Be sure to put a drain hole, or a pair of them, in the bottom.

Great mysteries explained!
(1) Bonsai soil is made up of three ingredients that you can find not far from your back door. (2) Repotting needn't be done every year. (3) Roots aren't half as delicate as they're made out to be. (4) Not all bonsai are grown in containers. (5) Keeping your trees happy and healthy involves no more effort and much less time each day than reading the morning paper.

A bonsai collection that speaks of good care. Ample space between plants for air, light allows them visual freedom.

A Certain Amount of Care

THERE IS A PREVAILING opinion that bonsai get that way from being starved — that they are under-nourished, neglected, twisted, tweaked, and otherwise tormented into submission.

This is far from fact. No plant could survive such treatment. Any living thing needs a minimum amount of nourishment to remain alive. With just a little more than minimum, a plant will survive, but barely. Its foliage may be sparse, its color sickly. If a plant is to be really healthy, it needs to be fed well and given a little tender care.

As important as feeding is attention to one or two other areas that influence the well-being of your trees. A bonsai that is overrun with weeds or pests won't be able to hold its own no matter how well it's fed. A bonsai that never has its roots or its foliage thinned won't have a good balance between top and bottom growth.

Some bonsai experts cut back roots as often as the plant will stand it, "to make more room for fresh soil." They feed their plants heavily, well, and often, and spend every spare minute of their time fussing around with the underpinnings of their trees.

Others seldom cut back roots. They maintain that top pruning is sufficient, that a plant will not become potbound if only the foliage is thinned, since a tree develops no more roots than the top requires. They cut roots initially only to get a plant into a pot, then nevermore touch the base.

Whatever the reasons, whether to prevent a plant from getting potbound or to allow roots to fit into a container or to permit more room for earth, the results are the same. The plant gets more nourishment and is a better plant for it. However you cut it, it's still cake — or, in this case, bonsai.

There are several often-heard questions regarding the care of bonsai. Most of them reflect a concern over just what is required in the way of care and what the benefit is. Here are a few.

Are branches and foliage cut back to make bonsai smaller? Yes, but this is not the only reason. Pinching back encourages healthy new growth. Branch pruning shapes a plant, but it also allows air and sunlight to reach foliage that might otherwise suffer from lack of it.

Are roots cut back to enable a large plant to be fitted into a small container? Yes, but more important, root cutting allows new feeder roots to grow and thus helps the plant obtain more nourishment.

Are plants periodically repotted because they get potbound? Yes, but repotting also replaces compacted soil and thus improves drainage and root aeration.

Are bonsai delicate things that have to be tended and looked after as a young child? Not at all. Aside from the time required in initially preparing a new plant for bonsai life, only a few minutes a day will suffice to keep even a large group of plants in good health.

Bonsai are not demanding in their needs, but they do need a certain amount of care.

When Should a Bonsai Be Repotted?

Root pruning keeps the root system within the bounds of the container and encourages the growth of fine feeder roots. Both results improve drainage and aeration. Both are conducive to the plant receiving better nourishment. The finer the roots, the more of them can be contained in the pot without crowding. The more root surface, without crowding, the better the plant is fed.

Don't worry about your plants becoming potbound. If they have been potted properly at the outset, and you have given the foliage proper attention, the roots will pretty much take care of themselves.

One professional bonsai grower has a stock answer when asked if he ever touches the roots of his plants. He grabs the trunk of a bonsai, lifts it and the entire root ball out of the container, and puts the tip of one finger against the roots.

"That's the only way I touch them," he says.

His point seems to be well made. Of his hundreds of handsome plants, not one seems to be suffering from having been left in the container too long.

A tree can easily be checked for a potbound condition. Around January or February, let the plant go

Typical root ball of many gallon-container plants. Look for circling or tightly tangled roots. Above plant is more than ready for transfer to new container.

Here's a really potbound plant. There is no soil left for roots, and if planted as is, the root ball would dry out faster than the surrounding soil.

An ideal root ball. Note the many fine root hairs, the absence of circling roots, good balance between roots and soil. This root ball needs little trimming.

Container should be matched to plant before repotting is started. All three of the potential bonsai shown here came from nursery. Can you identify finished plantings (lodgepole pine, Colorado blue spruce, maples) elsewhere in book?

without water for a day, so the soil will dry out. Hold the container firmly with one hand, and, grasping the trunk with the other, lift it gently out of the pot. Be sure you don't jerk it out. Look at the root system. If it's packed tightly in the form of the inside of the pot and there seems to be no space at all in the root mass for soil, then the plant is probably crowded and should be repotted. If there seems to be a fair amount of breathing space between roots, or if you can see only a few roots in the soil, then all is well.

This apparently rough treatment does no harm to the plant. Of course, you can't do this with a tree that is growing in a rock, or one that has several rocks around its base. With these, inspect the edges of the soil, or the drain holes in the bottom of the container, every year or so. If you see a *lot* of roots poking out (not just one or two), it's a fair sign that things are getting a little crowded.

Some examples of what to expect when you have a tree out of its container are given on pages 54 and 58.

Soil Is No Mystery

One of the most curious aspects of bonsai is their ability to grow in a minimum of soil. Many plants are potted in deep containers, but many highly prized specimens of great size and age are cultivated in trays only an inch or two deep. Others have a great part of their root system exposed and still others have their roots buried in the cracks of a rock.

No matter how much care a tree is given, it won't survive unless it has the right amount of moisture and good drainage. In the care and culture of bonsai these two factors are of paramount importance. Plants have been grown — and quite well — merely in a mixture of damp gravel and sand. The composition of the potting medium is of less importance than its ability to hold the right amount of moisture.

If you ever undertook to make a list of recommended soil mixes for bonsai use, you would find your task never-ending. Every person who works with bonsai, whether expert or novice, has his own pet formula. Each varies a bit depending on personal taste, on geographical area, on a dozen other influences. There are as many soil mixes for bonsai as there are bonsai fanciers. All of them — the mixes, that is — seem to work, but many of them become a bit complex in their compounding and formulation. Some require special clay, sand, peat moss, leaf mold, and such. Some call for screenings several times, moistening, and dehydrating. Small wonder that to the beginner such operations can make bonsai culture appear fearful.

Japanese black pine *(Pinus thunbergii)* around 30 years old. The rough trunk contributes to aged look. Exposed roots repeat twisted lines of branches. Compare this tree with Japanese red pine on page 74, which is three times as old.

Fortunately, the choice and use of soil can be as simple as any other aspect of bonsai culture.

The best soil for a particular tree is, logically enough, the soil in which that tree grows in its normal environment. Since it's usually not practical to have a supply of native soil for each of several varieties of trees, some compromise must be made.

The basic mix

The simplest mix seems to work just as well as the more involved ones and is little trouble to prepare and use. Basically, it contains sand, leaf mold, and earth. By sand is meant river or quarry sand. You can buy it from lumber yards, quarries, or even from variety stores (under the name of white aquarium sand). Don't use beach sand. It contains too much salt, and even if you wash it thoroughly, it's usually too fine. Sand provides no nourishment. It does provide aeration.

Leaf mold is available from any nursery in bags ranging from a couple of cupfuls to several cubic feet.

Leaf mold (you can use peat moss instead) also increases the air- and moisture-holding capacity of the soil and keeps it from compacting.

By earth is meant just plain old garden dirt. You get it by going outside and taking up some of Mother Earth. It should not contain large chunks of clay or rock, nor should it have too many grass roots or weeds. Don't use earth from a richly fertilized area, such as a vegetable garden; it might be too rich for bonsai.

For the basic mix the three ingredients are in equal proportions. Whether you make up a potful at a time or a washtubful, use ⅓ sand, ⅓ leaf mold, ⅓ earth. Put all the ingredients together and mix well with a garden trowel or your hands. Crush and blend in any dirt lumps, and pick out twigs or rocks larger than a pea. That's all there is to it.

This mix can be used for any bonsai. In fact, you can use it for any container plant, inside the house or outside. No exotic materials are needed. No screening is necessary. The soil will not compact and it won't hold too much water.

Drainage control

Earth should not be used by itself. It's usually too dense and with watering in a bonsai container will become compacted. Eventually it can become hard and water won't even penetrate the surface. The tiny feeder rootlets will be damaged and the tree will die back.

On the other hand, don't use leaf mold, or peat moss, alone. It will forever remain fluffy, and water will either run off the surface, or, if it does soak in, not stay long enough to do any good.

There are two refinements to the basic formula that will save you time in watering your bonsai. By a slight change in the proportions of the ingredients you can control the drainage for conifers, which need a slightly drier soil, and broad-leafed plants which require more moisture. This allows all plants to be watered together, and they will drain or hold water as they need it.

For Conifers: Use ½ sand; ¼ leaf mold; ¼ earth. This allows fast drainage.

For Broad-leaf Plants: Use ¼ sand; ¼ leaf mold; ½ earth. This allows slow drainage.

Potting and Repotting

Many people approach potting and repotting with fear and trembling. Just as some feel that it is sacrilegious to wire and bend the branches of a plant, others hesitate to touch the roots because it seems to be tampering with nature's ways. Others are just plain afraid of harming the plant. Once a plant is ready to be repotted, however, it is *ready*. Too long a delay may weaken the tree.

Here again, the best way to learn is to practice. Start with an inexpensive one-gallon nursery plant (such as a firethorn or a juniper). If you make a mistake and the plant expires, don't consider the loss a personal one. You will have learned something in the process. Such a plant is accustomed to crowded conditions and undoubtedly will be more than ready for repotting. Almost anything you do will be to its benefit.

🌲 Holes in a Ceramic Container

Some plain, unadorned ceramic containers make handsome bonsai pots. However, they must allow water to drain out of the soil. Drain holes should be at least ½ inch in diameter. With a little care and an electric drill you can bore a hole in almost any material.

Glass: Build up a small clay well around the area where the hole is to be. Sprinkle some powdered carborundum in the well and drill the hole with a copper tube clamped in the drill chuck.

Glazed Ceramic: Build up a clay well, put a little water in it, and use a carbide-tipped bit (available from any hardware store). Or use a copper tube and carborundum, as for glass.

Unglazed Pottery: Use a carbide-tipped bit.

Roots of this fir tree were circling the root ball. Such growth can cripple the tree if it continues its circling action. Snip off overly long roots.

Three large roots have started to circle the bottom of the nursery can. When planting in a deep bonsai container spread such roots or else cut them off short.

Have everything at hand

Always work away from direct sun and out of any wind, both of which tend to dry out exposed roots. If you plan to repot a nursery plant immediately, have the nurseryman cut the can. Otherwise, leave it uncut, since roots will dry out quickly. Your tools and materials should be handy so you don't have to dash off in the middle of the operation to find something. The following are the bare essentials.

Long knife or kitchen spatula, pruning shears, garden trowel.

A couple of chopsticks or other sticks about the size of a pencil, blunt at one end and sharpened at the other.

A bucket half full of water to which you've added about a tablespoon of liquid vitamin B_1 hormone.

The new container, with a piece of broken pottery over the drain hole, and about a third full of soil mix.

More than enough dry soil mix to fill the container when the plant is in it.

Sprinkling can or hose nozzle with a spray adjustment.

Moss, rocks, lichen, or whatever else you plan to use around the base of the potted tree.

Roots—what to look for

With a nursery container, if the can isn't cut, and you can't cut it yourself, slide a long knife blade down and around the inside of it to separate the root ball from the sides. Lift the plant gently by holding the trunk near the base. If it doesn't budge, turn the can upside-down and strike the edge on a hard surface, keeping one hand on the base of the plant to keep it from dropping free.

If you're repotting an established bonsai, remove any surface rocks and take off moss in pieces as large as possible. Keep the moss damp and use it again when you've repotted the tree. Hold the trunk firmly and rock it gently until the root ball comes free. Your job will be easier if you let the plant go without water the day before.

Inspect the root ball carefully. If you see only a few roots on the sides and bottom of the ball, treat it gently. Chances are that there aren't enough roots to hold the soil together. If the ball is webbed and matted with roots, treat it boldly, since in this case there are probably more roots than soil.

Just how much you prune the roots will depend on the condition of the ball. The objective is always the same. You want to encourage new roots to grow out into new surrounding soil as quickly as possible.

If the plant has several large roots that have started to circle the ball, cut them back by about a third, but leave most of the finer roots. If you find any long, thin roots encircling the root ball, unwind them first and snip them off entirely. If allowed to grow, they will eventually cripple the tree by their circling action.

Neither of the above examples represents a truly potbound plant. When you hoist the root ball of such a specimen, you'll recognize it at once. There will be little soil. The root mass will be compacted, solid to the touch. If you were to repot such a plant as is, even in a much larger container, the root ball would dry out faster than the surrounding soil and there would be little chance for new feeder roots to develop.

Keep roots from drying out

As soon as you have the plant out of the old container and have determined that the roots need attention, set the root ball in the bucket of vitamin enriched water. Sprinkle some of the water over the foliage, while letting the root ball soak for a couple of minutes.

Slosh the root ball around in the water, working it with your hands to wash old soil out from around the roots. Keep this up until most of the soil is cleared away. If necessary, use a pointed stick to help work out any hard soil, but be careful not to break too many of the fine rootlets.

Working the roots in water this way serves several purposes. Both the compacted earth and root ball are

softened, and the soil is washed out rather than having to be picked out, which might damage too many delicate roots. The roots are kept moist all the time. The vitamin B_1 starts work to stimulate the growth of new root systems. The liquid helps make the roots flexible, which will aid you in pruning them and arranging them later.

Clear the roots of as much soil as possible without belaboring them too long. It's not absolutely necessary that you clean away every particle of old soil. A little left in the center of the root mass will do no harm.

Trimming the roots

Lift the plant out of the water and separate the roots as well as you can. You may have to comb them out with your fingers or use a pointed stick. The main thing is to spread out winding or spiraling roots so you can get an idea of their length.

Now for the operation that most people shy away from. Cut away about a third of the total root mass, trimming smoothly around and under. Try to flatten the root mass on the bottom and round it on the edges. If the taproot extends downward, or is bent and wound, cut it back by two-thirds or even a little more. Be sure to slant the cut on the taproot — don't make it squarely across. As you do the trimming, dunk the roots occasionally in the water to wash away the loose ones and keep the remaining ones wet.

Roots must not be allowed to dry out while you're working on them. Wash dirt away in vitamin-enriched water, dunk roots frequently while pruning them.

Don't be hesitant about cutting back roots. Each cut root means that many more new rootlets will develop to provide more nourishment for the plant.

To keep soil from washing through container bottom, place a piece of wire mesh or broken pot over drain hole. Water must still be able to seep through.

Before settling plant in its container and firming soil around it, try different placements to find the best location and the one "right" tree orientation.

If you are potting a tree from a balled specimen, or one you have had in the ground, and it has a large taproot, handle it in the following way. Don't cut back all of the taproot at one time. Take off about a third, then the next time you repot take another third, and so on.

In your trimming, if there are thick, well developed roots that you plan to expose above the surface, make sure you don't cut into or nick these. Extraneous surface roots can be cut away as long as you don't destroy too many principal ones that support small feeder roots.

Peat Pot Potting

You may sometimes find a handsome bonsai possibility that has been grown in a peat pot. Should you plant the peat pot and all? Or should you take the roots out of the pot before repotting?

A well watered plant in a peat pot will have small roots growing out of the sides and bottom. In this case you plant pot and all right in the bonsai container and break away about an inch of the pot's rim. There will be little or no setback and the rest of the peat will be gradually assumed into the soil. If the peat pot is bone dry, with no roots grown into or through the sides, it needs special handling. Here, it's best to carefully crack the pot and peel it away. Plant only the root ball, after gently separating the roots.

Into the container

Once the root ball has been reduced to your satisfaction, put the plant into the prepared container. Some experts put a layer of gravel on the bottom of a container before adding any soil. They claim it helps to keep water from sitting on the bottom of the pot. Others believe this hinders drainage. If your soil mix is properly laced with sand and leaf mold, and you have a stone or piece of screen (plastic or some other noncorroding material) over the drain hole, this won't be necessary and you'll avoid all the controversy.

Settle the trimmed root mass into the soil, holding the plant steady with one hand. If the base of the trunk is a little below the rim of the container, you're ready to add soil around the roots. If it comes above the rim, take a little mix out from under the roots to make the plant sit lower. Remember that after potting and watering, the soil and the plant will settle somewhat and be a bit lower than they are now.

You can support the plant with one hand and add soil around and on top of the roots with the other. If you need both hands to work with, or if the tree is to be planted at an angle, it might be better to support it by wiring the root ball to the container.

Spread the roots out, flattening them and arranging them symmetrically around the base of the tree. Sprinkle more soil around and over the roots until they're covered, and press it down so it fills all the spaces between the roots. Again be careful not to break too many root hairs. A good way to settle the earth is to bump the container gently down on the work top from time to time.

Some experts recommend poking soil around the

roots with a chopstick. This should be done very carefully, since vigorous jabbing may break delicate roots.

After the container is filled to the rim or a little below, and all roots have been well covered, press down the surface with your hands. You can thump it gently with the side of a fist to help pack it, or pat it with the blade of the garden trowel.

If heavy roots are to be exposed above the surface, be sure to press soil under and around them, after arranging them. A root that stubbornly refuses to lie flat and be covered with dirt shouldn't be cut off in mid-air. If it's an expendable root, clip it close to the base of the tree and discard it. If it's necessary for proper root balance, pin it down with a length or two of stiff wire bent into a hairpin shape. Any tiny root hairs that stick up above the surface can be clipped back.

If after the plant is potted it still seems unstable, which it may be if it is a slanted or cascaded style, you can tie it to the pot. Run three or four guy wires or lengths of twine from the trunk at about the first main branch out to the edge of the pot. Secure the wires around the pot, and leave them there for a couple of months, or until the tree becomes stabilized. They will be unsightly, but only temporarily. Be sure you don't fasten the wires too tightly to the trunk or they may scar it.

The "best" location

Before beginning any potting, or even root trimming, you should plan just how you're going to arrange the tree in the new pot. You should decide beforehand if it will be upright, slanted, cascaded, or whatever. Don't wait until you have the tree settled in soil, then change your mind and try to reorient it.

If you're potting a new bonsai — that is, putting a tree into a bonsai container for the first time — you're fairly free in setting its attitude then. However, if you're repotting an already established form, think twice before changing it to a radically different style. Certain changes *can* be made without disrupting the harmony of the tree. You can separate a group of trees to plant them as individuals. You can change a slanted style to a cascaded style by planting it at a greater angle or wiring it lower. You can plant several small trees together to make a clump.

But be careful about making an abrupt change. A tree that has had some training as a cascade, for example, would hardly lend itself to an abrupt change to an upright form. The radical shaping that would be required for such a change might do harm to the tree.

In placing a tree in a rectangular or oval container, you should locate the base of the tree about a third of the distance from one end and slightly to the back. If the container is square, hexagonal, or round, the

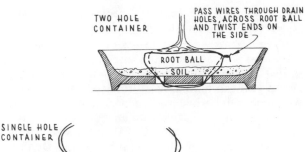

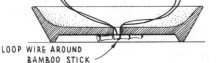

Two ways to secure bonsai in a container. Cover the wires with soil or with moss. They can remain in the container until the tree is ready for repotting.

Large surface roots are pinned down with a "U" shaped piece of wire. You can use part of a paper clip or even a large hairpin. Cover wire with soil or moss.

Use sharp scissors or small pruning shears to trim off small roots that stick up after the soil is firmed. If left, they make base of tree look unkempt.

tree can go in the center, except for the cascaded style, which should be planted a little off-center.

If you're arranging a grove of trees, handle and plant one tree at a time. Make sure each is firmly settled before planting the next one. With a tight clump you can hold several trees together fairly well with one hand while adding and tamping soil with the other. An alternative is to anchor the roots to the underlying soil with lumps of damp adobe or thick mud which you then cover with more soil. Don't use too much mud, since it cuts off air from the roots.

The finishing touches

Once you have the soil packed down and the tree is stabilized, use a sprinkling can or the fine spray adjustment on a hose nozzle for watering. Wet the foliage thoroughly, and water the soil several times, letting the water soak in and run out the drain hole. The last time you can use the vitamin enriched water from the bucket. Don't let the water form rivulets or wash the soil away.

Another way to soak a newly potted plant is to let it sit in a tub of water for about 10 minutes, during which time the water will come up through the drain holes. The water level in the tub should not be above the top edge of the bonsai container.

While the surface is still wet, place any rocks that are to be part of the arrangement, firming soil around them and settling them in.

If you are going to use sand or gravel on the surface, let the soil drain before adding it. If moss is to be the cover, lay irregular pieces on the damp soil, fitting them together as with a jigsaw puzzle. Cover all of the surface, even under exposed roots. Press the moss down gently with your fingers. When it is all down and pressed into place, sprinkle the surface again. Watering it a couple times a day for the first week will keep the moss green and help it to become anchored on the soil.

If you use dried and pulverized moss (see page 64), sprinkle it over damp soil, press it, and water it. It will become green in no time.

When the tree is completed, keep it in a shady place for about a week. Don't fertilize it for at least a month.

Aiding the Illusion

The surface of a bonsai planting should seldom be absolutely flat. A smooth, level, green surface looks more like a pool table than a pasture. In firming the soil down and adding moss, make little mounds, hillocks, and hollows to break the monotony and give more interest to the planting as a whole. Bonsai are intended to duplicate a natural situation or scene.

Accessories also should be natural and arranged in a natural manner.

Rocks give stability

Using rocks properly is one of the best ways of establishing a scene and adding a natural feel to a bonsai planting. Insofar as possible, the type of rock and its form and habit should match that of the type of tree and its environment.

Of course, no one can take the time to learn every possible rock form that would accompany every type of tree. It's sufficient to know a couple of general types and how to use them.

Most pines, spruce, and other evergreens live in the company of fairly rugged rock forms. These rocks have straight edges, jagged tops, and often deep clefts. Such rocks should appear to thrust up out of the earth. They shouldn't lie flat, as if scattered around on the surface. Trees should seem to grow out of them or around them; the rocks shouldn't lean tiredly against a trunk.

If you use several such rocks, either in a group or scattered, try to keep their "grain" running in the same direction. They should appear to be part of the same geological formation rather than objects poked here and there with no relation to each other or to the tree.

Lower altitude trees, such as oaks and maples, often grow in the company of rocks that are somewhat rugged, but have considerably softer contours. Volcanic stones are well suited for this type of bonsai. They are pitted and pocked, and their shapes have good character. Their rough texture harmonizes with the shaggy bark of certain trees, and offers good contrasts with others that are smooth.

Trees whose habitat is in the lowlands or near water are usually in the company of smoother stones. Here especially, watch that the rocks don't seem to be just lying around. They should follow some natural form both in their attitude and their arrangement. Clump odd numbers of them together, or use a couple of large ones in company with a smaller one for contrast.

Rocks are as easy to find as dirt — look under your feet. Any hike, camping trip, or vacation drive should yield a few rocks with interesting forms. Add them to your collection even though at the moment of finding you have no specific arrangement in mind.

Caution: Some State and National Parks forbid taking rocks as well as plant material. Make sure you're in the right before collecting.

Stone yards, brick yards, garden and landscaping centers, and some nurseries are good commercial sources for rocks. A type of volcanic material called feather rock or foam rock has many bonsai uses. It's extremely lightweight; it's soft and can be chipped and gouged easily.

Three trees of different sizes form the nucleus of a grove. They are arranged, then trimmed lightly for general form and design before rest of the planting.

When placement is decided, anchor trees on layer of soil mix with lumps of damp mud or adobe placed between roots under base of trunk. Don't use too much.

Locate rest of trees in same manner as first three, add soil around roots, and firm it in. Remove crossing branches and trim rest to unify entire planting.

Mound soil up irregularly for greater interest (it can be higher at one end of the container), add moss, and water either from bottom up or by sprinkling.

Don't use highly polished stones. In a bonsai planting they have an air of artificiality. Beach rocks can be used, but they should be soaked in fresh water for several weeks to rid them of salt and alkali that might be harmful to plants.

In arranging rocks, never use an even number. More interest is created with one, three, or five stones than with two or four. An even number seems to make a statement that is final and balanced — one that leaves no room for further participation. For the same reason, vary the sizes of rocks if several are used.

Two different types of rock can be used together if arranged with a definite and apparent purpose. They shouldn't be mixed randomly.

Moss and other greenery

Soft green moss beneath the branches of a potted tree adds another touch of life to a bonsai planting. A healthy layer of moss also helps to conserve moisture in the container, and is a good indicator of the condition of the soil. If the moss looks hard and is brown, it and the soil beneath it are probably in need of water. If the moss is soft and green, the moisture content of the soil is good.

Where can you get moss for your bonsai? Moss is found not so much on the north side of trees but in damp areas that receive little direct sun. In early spring, when the weather is wet, look on the shady sides of garden stones. The edges of brick patios often develop a feathery coating of moss. Even in cities, moss frequently will grow along the edges of curbs during prolonged rains. You'll find it on large rocks out in the woods, along river banks, on damp retaining walls — almost any moist spot that doesn't receive much sun.

In gathering heavy moss, slide a blade under it and lift it in pieces as large as possible. By the time you get it home it may be dry and brown, but it will revive. Lay the pieces out in a wooden flat or spread them in a cool corner of the garden. With daily watering it will stay green and will grow.

You can also scrape up moss when it's dry. Pulverize it and store the powder in an open container in a dry place. Don't worry if a little clinging soil gets mixed in. Use the powder instead of moss chunks, as described on page 62.

Zelkova with an otherwise uninteresting form is enhanced by the addition of rocks, moss, and by leaving some of the roots exposed. Tree is 20 years old.

Very young deodar cedar, in early stages of training as a cascaded bonsai, has pale green lichen anchored on top of moss with a hairpin.

Under proper conditions of good shade and watering, many bonsai will develop a thin moss on their trunks. This is fairly common with the pines. This in no way affects a tree but gives it a more aged look. Also, fungi (toadstools) may sprout on the surface of a planting during a wet spring. These aren't harmful either and they add a nice touch.

Lichens and liverworts — green relatives of mosses and fungi — can be collected and used with bonsai. They provide a bit more of nature. Over a period of a year or more, however, keep an eye on them, and tear them back if they seem to be growing too much.

Dichondra, baby's tears, Irish moss, and other tiny-leafed ground covers add character to a bonsai planting, either by themselves or in the company of moss. If they start overgrowing the moss or covering rocks completely, thin them out. Some of the small grasses and ferns add a nice touch. Be sure to check with your nursery as to their growth habits, and avoid any that get too big or grow too fast.

Rock Plantings Need Special Attention

There are two types of rock plantings whose potting and repotting calls for techniques a bit different from those used for a regular container planting. Also, a different soil mix is used to help anchor roots to rocks until growth in the soil is well developed. This is called peat muck, and it's made as follows.

Mix peat moss and earth in the ratio of six parts of peat to four parts of earth. Wet the mixture thoroughly, then press out all extra water. Don't let this mix dry out while you're using it.

On the rocks

With the aid of peat muck, small trees can be grown entirely on a rock that is not in any kind of a pot. The rock itself serves as a container, and it suggests an entire landscape. The roots grow in the muck within hollows of the rock.

Choose a very rough rock with several good-sized pockets in it that will give ample space for soil and roots. Or use a chunk of feather rock in which you've gouged a hole. While cleaning the roots of the tree, let the rock soak in the vitamin enriched water. Prune the roots very lightly, removing only about a fourth of the total mass, including any very long ones.

Press some peat muck into the principal cavity and any lesser hollows near it. The muck will stick if it's been wet properly. Now arrange the tree as you wish it to be right on top of the muck, and pack more muck around the roots.

Flat rock planting of a lodgepole pine. Such bonsai must be handled carefully in order that tree and its root system do not become separated from the rock.

When all of the roots are covered, press moss over the muck. Tie the whole thing together — rock, moss, and tree — by binding it with light wire, twisted raffia, or string. Spray with water, being careful not to wash any muck out from under the moss.

Keep the bonsai in a shady spot for a couple of weeks, watering it very often, since rock plantings can dry out fast. Frequently, this type of planting is set permanently in a low tray with water or wet sand. After a couple of months, or when the moss starts growing, you can take the wire off. Be careful that you don't joggle the tree loose.

Over the rocks

Another type of rock planting has the rock sitting in a soil-filled container. The tree, in turn, sits on the rock, with its roots exposed and running down into the soil.

Prepare a container as for a regular planting, filling it about three-fourths with basic soil mix. Have moist peat muck made up and ready. Soak the rock on which the tree is to be planted, while cleaning and straightening the roots. *Do not trim any of the roots.*

Plaster muck all along the sides of the rock. Set

Dwarf pomegranate (*Punica granatum* 'Nana') with roots exposed over a piece of black volcanic rock. Pebbles and baby tears make up the rest of the base.

Good arrangement of rocks on top of moss adds dimension to shallow container, ties it in with conifer. Long axis of rocks follows long axis of container.

the tree on the rock, and arrange the roots over the muck and down the rock and under it. Settle the rock in the container. Bury about a quarter of the rock in soil (not muck), making sure the ends of the roots are well covered.

Now cover the roots that are on the rock with muck, and wire or tie all together, as above. You can add moss to the surface of the soil in the container, but don't put any over the muck since it will be removed later.

After about a year the roots will have established themselves in the soil of the pot. You can then untie the plant and carefully wash away the peat muck from the rock, leaving the bare roots hugging the bare rock.

Again, through its early growth, this type of planting needs careful and frequent watering. Use a very fine spray on the peat muck in order that you don't wash it off too soon.

Keeping Your Trees Happy

There's not a great deal that need be done to keep bonsai healthy and happy, once they've been potted properly. It boils down pretty much to good watering, occasional feeding, a little winter attention, and watching for pests.

Don't neglect watering

Much can be and is made of the esoterics of watering bonsai. One often reads that only distilled water should be used, that an inflexible schedule should be followed, that trees must be watered from the bottom up, and so on.

The watering of bonsai is no more difficult nor complicated than any other aspect of their care. The only rule here is that they must not be allowed to remain dry over a long period. When a plant is dry, you give it a drink, and that's about all there is to it. Keeping your plants in shade or semi-shade and out of the wind will help in keeping them from drying out.

Even in very hot areas, a single watering each day is usually enough. Bonsai should not be constantly saturated. Even if the moss on the surface of a plant looks a little brown, as long as the plant itself appears green and rich and there is no sign of wilting, it's probably happy. Too much water can do just as much harm as not enough.

The best time to water is either the first thing in the morning or the last thing at night. When you water in the evening, the plants hold their moisture longer, since they have several hours before the sun starts heating the air around them. If you water in the morning, do it before the sun gets too high and too hot, since the leaves of some trees (maples, in particular) may spot if they have water and then sun on them.

Special sprinkling cans aren't necessary. A good hose nozzle that can be adjusted to a fine spray works well. Your thumb over the end of an open hose is also a fine device.

When watering, direct a light spray over the base of the plants, let it soak in, then come back and do it again. The surface should be well saturated, and, ideally, water should run out of the drain holes in the bottom of the container.

Direct a harder stream over all the foliage, but not so hard that it will injure delicate leaves. This knocks off many insects and cleans the leaves of soot and other dirt.

In some areas, particularly in the southern United States, tap water is a bit alkaline for bonsai. Rain water can be collected and stored for such potted plants instead. Unless the water in your area presents such problems, use it right from the hose. Your local nursery can tell you about the condition of the water.

In large metropolitan areas, smog may affect some broadleaf plants. Some maples leaf out in the spring all right, but before long the leaves will start turning brown at the edges, then shrivel altogether. In such areas, the Japanese white pine, the Japanese holly, the beech, and spruce usually do poorly. There's little that can be done except to keep the foliage as clean as possible.

Some bonsai fanciers water their plants from the bottom by setting the container in a large pan of water until the soil becomes saturated. This can be a lot of trouble, especially if you have a dozen or more plants to handle. Also, it sometimes tends to cause an accumulation of alkali salts in the bottom of the container.

The most trying time for a bonsai is when its owner is on vacation. There are two ways to keep your trees healthy when you're away from them for prolonged periods. You can have a reliable neighbor water them daily. Or you can sink the pots in the ground (almost to the rim) and have an unreliable neighbor water the entire garden once or twice a week. An advantage in being acquainted with others who are interested in bonsai is that you can trade off watering during vacation times.

Feeding is essential

Since a bonsai is a living plant — even though a miniature one — it needs nourishment for life. A bonsai could survive for a year, possibly longer, with

Owner of these trees—a professional bonsai grower—prefers to keep his conifers together for special watering, feeding.

Note that each tree, whatever its form, is "right" for its container. The tree third from the right is over 200 years old.

no more food than what is in the soil, but it won't look its best and will not be as healthy as it would with good feeding. Proper feeding satisfies the needs of a plant for food, promotes rich growth, and helps the plant to resist disease.

Almost any house plant food will work well for bonsai, as long as it's not used too strongly. Some plant food comes in the form of pills or tablets that you put on the surface or press into the soil and let dissolve with watering. Liquid fertilizers, such as fish oil emulsion, should be used according to the directions given on the bottle. These ready mixes are much easier to use than exotic formulas of steeped chicken manure or ground abalone, and they do just as good a job. Don't use dry fertilizers or manure — they are too strong for bonsai.

In diluting a commercial plant food, don't make a richer solution than is called for in the directions on the box or bottle. As mild as house plant foods are, they can harm a delicate bonsai if used too strongly. It's better to overdilute than to underdilute.

Use a small sprinkling can to apply liquid fertilizer, and saturate the soil thoroughly until water comes out the drain hole. Don't get fertilizer on foliage; it may burn.

The chart on pages 78 and 79 shows the best times to fertilize. In general, flowering trees are fed in the spring, and most others in the autumn. In the spring, as soon as new buds appear and while the leaves are opening, fertilize every other week. After the leaves are fully open, and throughout the summer, a monthly feeding will suffice. Then during September and October, feed every other week. Don't feed bonsai during mid-winter.

Winter care

In many parts of the western United States winter means little change in care of bonsai. For those persons fortunate enough to live in areas that have mild winters, frequent rains, and occasional sunlight, bonsai are cared for by the elements themselves, and actually need less attention than they do during the rest of the year.

If your trees have some kind of shelter overhead — even the foliage of a spreading tree — frosts will seldom bother them. About all you have to watch for is that the soil doesn't dry out and stay that way.

Where winters are severe, bonsai care is another story. Although they do need more attention, they needn't be pampered. Even in the hardest winters bonsai should not be kept in a greenhouse or too warm a place. You may force unseasonal growth, and bonsai need a good rest period. Good air circulation is more important than warmth.

If you have some sort of lathhouse arrangement for your trees, put up side shelters during the winter that will help protect from frost but will still allow fresh air movement. In Japan, wooden frames with straw matting are used. Inexpensive roll-up bamboo blinds will work, as long as you brace them against strong winds.

You can build a simple coldframe by digging a hole about a foot and a half deep in the earth, making it as long and as wide as you need for all of your plants. (Do this *before* the ground is frozen; it's much easier.) Line the sides but not the bottom with exterior grade plywood, which should extend 6 inches above the surface. Put 4 to 6 inches of gravel in the bottom of the hole, set your containers on the gravel, then spread straw around and over them. Put a loose fitting top on the frame, made with old window glass panes or polyethylene sheeting that will let in light. (For other coldframe ideas and plans see the *Sunset* books, *Basic Gardening Illustrated* and *Garden Work Centers*.)

Coldframe kits are available that are both inexpensive and easy to assemble. Check with local nurseries or see the catalogs of mail order garden supply houses.

During cold winter months water your trees in the morning. This allows the water to drain out during the day. If water stands in the soil at night and freezes, it may crack the container.

Weeds and other pests

In addition to keeping an eye on the general health of your trees, you should watch for the growth of weeds in the container. Weeds detract from the appearance of a plant and can make a good bonsai look very messy. They also rob the soil of nourishment that should go to the tree.

Whenever you walk past your plants, take a quick glance at them. If you see a weed sprouting, take a second or two to pull it up right then and there. Keep the surface clean and free of dead leaves or pine needles by picking them off or brushing them away. Be careful not to tear up any moss.

Dead leaves on the surface of a bonsai can harbor insects — another good reason for not letting them accumulate.

The most common bonsai pests are aphids, red spider mites, scale insects, snails, slugs, sowbugs, pillbugs, and earwigs. Most insects are quickly and effectively dealt with by giving foliage a gentle blast with the hose when watering. A little snail bait scattered around the area will help too. Don't leave bonsai sitting directly on the ground for too long. Sowbugs and earwigs will congregate under the container.

If pests get ahead of you and start riddling the leaves of your favorite maple or gnawing into the bark of your best pine, check with a nursery for a good spray for either specific or all-around use.

Why is a bonsai? To many persons, miniature potted trees are many things. But to all, bonsai are an endless source of varied pleasure. Raising them is fun; using them is enjoyable. They can add subtle touches in the garden and they can be important decorative elements in the house. There are good bonsai and there are not-so-good bonsai. The aim of individual enthusiasts as well as organized clubs is to make better and better bonsai.

Bonsai, like other treasures, deserve thoughtful display. The mesh tops on the stands above permit good air circulation.

What Do You Do With Them?

JUST WHICH ASPECT of bonsai provides the most pleasure is debatable. In searching out likely specimens you experience the fun of discovering a handsome plant plus that of anticipating what you can do with it when you get it home. In propagating, by any of the straightforward methods presented earlier, there is the pleasure of bringing something out of next to nothing. In potting and establishing a tree there is the enjoyment of making a new form — in this case, making a miniature living tree out of what might be a plain, ordinary plant.

Even the daily care of bonsai affords a great deal of satisfaction. The results are slow. You may live with a tree for months before any changes are evident. But after conscientious watering and feeding and pinching back you'll one day see the first pale green tips of new growth and know that the tree is not only living but thriving. Then you'll have real evidence that your efforts haven't been in vain.

But this isn't the end of pleasure. When the creation is done with, and the plant is pretty much taking care of itself, you don't just let it occupy space.

A bonsai then becomes something to live with. Unlike a flower bed or border, it's a permanent part of a home. With proper care it will in all likelihood outlive its owner.

As soon as you discover how very easy and enjoyable bonsai are, your collection will start to grow. What began as a tiny seedling in a miniature container will become a shelf of four or five junior-size trees. These in turn will develop into yet another shelf of larger and more handsome trees. As your interest and skill grow, so will your collection. You'll find that

Sturdy bonsai shelves for either work or display run in two directions, give three levels for plants of any size or shape. Details are given in text, page 71.

you are raising bonsai purely for the pleasure in handling a living plant form.

Then one day you'll be proudly showing your trees to a friend, and he'll ask, "But what do you do with them?" Or maybe when that small single plant has grown to a dozen or more, you'll step back and survey your shelves and ask yourself the same question.

First and Last . . . Enjoy Your Bonsai

Bonsai are meant to be enjoyed. From the inception of the idea for a possible form to the tree itself many seasons and years later, a bonsai is an object of enjoyment.

Inside or outside, miniature trees can be enjoyed at all times, regardless of the season of year or the hour of the day. The growth habits of each tree makes it something special, even if you have a wide variety of species. Evergreens display their rich green throughout the year. Flowering trees put on their best show in the spring or early summer. Deciduous trees provide clusters of color during the autumn. Fruiting trees are especially charming at bearing times. Trees with good branch and trunk forms invite admiration during the winter when their foliage is gone.

If you have more than a couple of trees, you should set up a shelf or two for handling and for displaying your prized specimens. Display shelves can be combined with a workbench, or can be entirely separate. You might want to have a few trees displayed in one area and keep others near the potting bench. Trees in process — plants you're giving special attention to, such as trees in training pots that have to be watched closely — should be fairly close to the work center.

You can scatter finished trees around the garden, but if your collection is at all sizeable, this will create problems in watering and general care. It's better to have a generally localized area where you can keep plants together, except for the few you may be using at any one time for display. All get equal care and none is likely to be overlooked.

All bonsai have the same basic requirements. They have to have water, light, and good air circulation. They shouldn't be jammed so close that they deprive each other, yet they needn't be spread out so much that care becomes a chore.

Leave about a foot of space between specimens, certainly no less than 6 inches, depending on the size of the trees. Let them have some sun (morning is best), especially in the spring when new growth is sprouting. In full shade, the leaves of most plants will be pale and weak. Turn the containers every couple of months to let all sides of the foliage have the full benefit of watering, reflected light, and air currents. In containers that aren't turned, roots tend to grow to the side that isn't heated by the sun. The foliage, however, reaches toward the source of strongest light.

Trees that are kept too close to a wall often will develop withered branches in the back.

You may want to group species — all pines together, all maples together, all flowering trees together, or some such arrangement. Or you may prefer to mix them any old way. Do keep the tallest trees in back of the shorter ones so none will miss its watering. Also, a tree that is hidden from view can't be enjoyed by others if you're the only one who knows it's there.

In the Garden

The simplest of shelves for holding or displaying bonsai can be made by setting a plank on two concrete blocks or some bricks. More elaborate set-ups are shown in photographs throughout this chapter and elsewhere in the book. By inspecting the pictures you'll see that the best arrangements are those that are kept simple. Rough lumber can be used, and the cruder the results, the better. It'll add to the character established by the trees.

You can build shelves against a shaded garage wall, against a fence, around a tree, or in many other such places in the garden. If you put several shelves against a wall, allow plenty of space between for good air circulation and so the tops of your trees won't be jammed down.

Free-standing shelves, such as those shown on page 39, should be stepped to prevent crowding. They should be at least a foot wide, which will suffice for most containers. Anything narrower is too narrow. It's easy and disastrous to slide a large container up onto a shelf and keep sliding it right off the back edge.

A handy arrangement is shown on page 70. The unit is basically a table-shelf that can be used for a work top. About 18 inches above the surface is a single shelf, for plants being worked on or finished trees. Between the legs of the table, resting on a cross member, is another shelf formed simply by a plank (it needn't be nailed down). The lower shelf is handy for empty containers or shade loving plants. The legs are made with 4 by 4-inch posts; the shelves are 2 by 10's or 2 by 12's; the supporting members are 2 by 4's. Such tables can be used individually or grouped.

In putting bonsai shelves against a light-colored outside wall away from trees, make sure they don't get too much sun. Between the direct sun's rays and those reflected from the wall, there can develop a great burning heat.

In addition to displaying your entire collection as a whole, you can group plants effectively in select outdoor areas. One owner uses his bonsai collection to bring some natural forms to a swimming pool area.

He uses a combination of raised stone beds and higher shelves against a wall at an end of the pool, all protected by a lathwork overhead. A caution to be observed in such a set-up: Don't let children water the trees from the swimming pool. The chemicals in the water are harmful to plants.

Slat benches and decks, either adjoining the house or in the garden, are good places for bonsai. They have somewhat of an oriental look about them that fits well with the containers and the trees. Also, the space between the boards allows good air circulation beneath the pots and permits drainage without forming a dark, inviting lair for insects.

Larger bonsai are often too massive to keep on a shelf with other trees. The total weight may be too much for a single plank and can crack it and dump all the trees in a tragic heap. If a shelf looks as if it's sagging in the middle, be sure to brace it. Remember that when plants have been freshly watered they are quite a bit heavier than when dry.

Big trees and containers usually look better displayed alone. Rather than setting a plant right on the earth, or on a green ground cover where it will leave a mark, use some kind of a stand.

A few used bricks can raise a container off the ground and away from pests. A flat rock makes a handsome stand. A very special bonsai deserves a special place for display. You can reserve a corner of a deck outside a large window, where the tree can be

Small collection of bonsai kept in one place. Shelves are held to fence by brackets, and a three-foot-wide lath extension overhead shades from direct sun.

Bonsai collection that is a decorative part of the garden provides a focal point for the area. Though no shelter is used, trees protect the plants.

enjoyed from inside the house as well as from the garden. You could use it as a fresh design element near the garden entry or the front door of the house where it will be seen by guests.

Large trees should be out and away from other greenery or walls that might create a confining influence. However, a wall or a panel located a little distance behind a tree will provide a plain background and will emphasize its artistic qualities.

Night lighting can be dramatic on a single tree or on a group of bonsai. Instead of shining a floodlight head-on, try back lighting to emphasize branch structure by silhouetting it or throwing a shadow.

Bonsai can usually be picked up and carried around for relocating. A big plant needs a little more care in moving, since it can be awkward to handle as well as heavy. Two people can move a large plant by lifting it onto some boards placed across a wheelbarrow. Then one trundles the wheelbarrow while the other steadies the plant. Another method is shown at the foot of this page. The container is moved on boards over three rollers (large wooden dowels, or large metal pipe). As you move the tree off one roller, transfer that roller to the front. This is a traditional Japanese technique for moving heavy plants short distances.

In the House

Bonsai are outdoor plants and should not be kept inside for more than two days. When they're in a house any longer, they suffer, since the interior is too warm and dry.

A few species can be kept indoors most of the year without harm. These are tropicals and subtropicals, plus some hardy species, that can be trained into a reasonable bonsai style. They are well suited to small apartments with no balcony space.

Pyracantha (firethorn), some azaleas, many cotoneasters, a few varieties of ivy, and hawthorn can be trained into house bonsai. Dwarf pomegranate (see the photo on page 66) makes a colorful plant, and has a good basic form for training. Gardenia, rosemary, camellia, Surinam cherry (*Eugenia uniflora*), Barbados cherry (*Malpighia glabra* — a tropical plant, growing in southern Texas and Hawaii), Singapore holly (*Malpighia coccigera* — also a tropical), common myrtle (*Myrtus communis*), and some bamboos are also adaptable to inside culture.

With either house bonsai or trees that you bring in for a day or two, don't set a specimen where it will receive direct sun, even through a window. Also, keep it away from hot air ducts and radiators. Don't overwater, but watch that indoor bonsai don't stay dry for long.

Before bringing a bonsai indoors, water it and let

Japanese black pine with three years of training. The stand is portable, is made from 1 by 1-inch garden stakes resting on 2 by 4-inch runners.

Platform made from ⅝-inch grooved external plywood displays a single pine against a lath fence. In the late afternoon the tree casts interesting shadows.

Traditional Japanese method for moving large container a short distance. One person pushes plant on boards over three rollers; other takes last roller to front.

Engawa, or wooden terrace, is an important architectural feature of many Japanese homes. Adapted to an American home, as shown above, it makes an ideal display area for a bonsai collection, visible from within house and from garden.

it drain well for a couple of hours. Wipe dirt and dampness from the container. Don't water it again while it's in the house, or the mat and stand on which it sits may become spotted.

Displaying your bonsai

In a traditional Japanese home — or a modern one that has even a little tradition carried into its design — there is an alcove known as a *tokonoma*. It is the most important part of a home in that works of art are exhibited there.

The *tokonoma* is basically a platform raised a few inches above the regular floor level, and is a little larger than 3 by 6 feet in area. It's usually in one corner of the living room. Paintings, decorative scrolls, and calligraphy are hung against the wall at the back. On the platform are placed a flower arrangement, a piece of ceramic ware, a bronze incense burner, a bonsai, or some other very special object that has aesthetic value.

Locating such objects in an area such as this gives them emphasis and draws attention to them. All of the above objects are not displayed together, since they would compete for attention, but certain of them are carefully chosen and arranged to complement one another or to emphasize one particular feature.

The same principal can be adapted to many areas in the home without the need for a *tokonoma*. For example, you can place a bonsai in front of a plain wall on a raised stand. On the wall, and a little to one side of the tree, you can hang a simple painting — one with colors that will not compete with any colors in the bonsai. Then you can add, on a lower stand, a fine piece of pottery. That's all — it's a simple grouping, but one that is effective.

An entry can be decorated with a bonsai by placing the tree against the far wall facing the entry, without hanging a painting on the wall. Such a plant should be a few inches below eye level, and should not be in the exact center of the wall area but a little to one side to give asymmetrical balance.

If you set a bonsai on a low stand or table, you can use a small Japanese folding screen behind it. A gold screen makes a good background for conifers; a silver screen looks good behind broadleaf trees.

Don't combine bonsai with flower arrangements. Both will be fighting for attention, and each will defeat the other. An object that is smaller than the bonsai and its container — such as an empty, plain pot — gives a secondary point of emphasis.

Bonsai classic—the Japanese red pine (*Pinus densiflora*)—trained in the slanted style. The needles are long and are bluish green. The dead branch at the left is purposely left on for special interest. This tree is over 80 years old.

Stands and mats

Stands made especially for flower arrangements or bonsai display can be found in Oriental stores. High tables are well suited for cascaded plants. The small low teak or rosewood tables with curved-under or stubby legs are good and can be found in stores that handle imported merchandise. A polished tree stump, with roots serving as legs and with a flat top, is expensive but is quite handsome and carries through the natural appearance of the bonsai that it supports.

In general, the shape of the top of the stand or table should contrast with the shape of the container, and the height of the stand should harmonize with the height of the tree. Thus, a long cascaded bonsai needs a high stand to allow full downward sweep of the foliage. A medium-height stand should be used for bonsai with straight, vertical trunks. Broad, low stands are best for a grove of trees or a windswept style tree.

A mat or pad is usually placed between the container and the stand. It protects the surface of the stand and blends tree and container in with the stand. Woven place mats, in plain colors, are used. Bamboo "raft" mats also look good with certain trees. A sliced cross section of some handsome wood — such as redwood — makes a good-looking mat.

Although purists would frown on the practice, bonsai can be decorated for festive occasions. Small ornaments, party favors, candies, origami birds, or other paper devices can be hung by threads from the branches of a small tree. The plant can then be used as a centerpiece for a table. Be sure to use lightweight objects that won't bend branches out of shape.

Bonsai make wonderful gifts. With just a little shaping you can transform a seedling or a nursery container plant into a lovely tree. In a soft-colored, glazed container, such a tree becomes a very special present.

When giving bonsai, be sure to tell the recipient how to care for his plant. Tell him it is definitely not an indoor plant (unless it is), and that it needs proper watering. He'll probably be happy if you check on it from time to time to make sure it's healthy.

What Is a Good Bonsai?

All manner of rules have been formulated for judging bonsai. Most of them are based on two considerations: health and beauty.

If a tree is healthy, it will look healthy. Deception is not possible, since a badly cared for plant will not have the rich foliage and the full branching of a healthy one. A tree that has been given good care will be free of weeds; there will be no brown or dead leaves on its branches. In the spring it will have fat buds or clean new growth. It will look as if it has been in the container for a long time so that both have become part of each other.

Thick, green moss is a good indicator that the plant has been long in a container. Brown, crisp moss can mean neglect in watering.

The soil must not be rock-hard, but still must be firm to the touch. A few tiny roots showing at the drain hole are evidence of good health and good growth.

A tree can be quite healthy but can still fail as a successful bonsai because it has no beauty. Overall form is perhaps the first thing that attracts the eye. There should be good balance between the foliage and the branches and trunk of a tree. The tree must be in good proportion to its container.

Wire marks on branches, or crude cuts caused by careless pruning, always detract from the value of a tree. Branches that have been cut short should have a natural look. The ends should seem as if they were damaged by some natural force rather than being left as squared-off stubs.

The front of a tree should face out. There should be no unsightly gaps in the foliage. The trained form of the tree should be in agreement with the species it duplicates — no cascaded redwoods, no formal upright fruit trees.

If you start going to bonsai shows or displays, you'll get to recognize old friends among the trees. The award winners show up year after year, and after seeing them a time or two you'll be able to tell just how much each has improved over the preceding year. This is the mark of excellence of an established tree that has reached maturity. Although exceedingly subtle, its changes from year to year are the key to its prize winning form.

At shows, bonsai are usually exhibited on long, cloth-covered tables. The trees are separated from one another by folding screens or partitions, although sometimes small trees may be grouped. At shows, as well as when viewing private collections of bonsai, the rule is *hands off the trees!* Too many people cannot look and admire without handling, and too many fine bonsai are ruined by persons pinching branches or poking rocks.

At shows you'll often see bonsai with a little roofed wooden signpost sticking out of the earth at the base of the tree. These signs list, in Japanese characters, the improvement the tree has shown since the last judging. Since they are complimentary to the plant, they are prized highly by owners.

Sharing the Bonsai Hobby

Bonsai clubs and societies have been formed in many areas of the country. They comprise a wide variety

Display shelf near entry holds a gnarled pine. This particular tree seems to fit no specific form, can only be termed grotesque. Therein lies its beauty.

Pinus contorta is forty years old. Tiny Christmas lights follow the graceful lines of its trunk and branches, make a festive and unusual tree.

of interested persons, from novices to old-timers who cultivate bonsai professionally. At periodic meetings members can exchange ideas and help each other. Meetings include workshops, lecture-demonstrations, and critiques. The more advanced members are very willing to teach beginners more about bonsai.

The following pages list most of the larger bonsai clubs in the West and Hawaii, and several in other regions of the country. It is possible that membership in some groups is presently filled and you may have to be placed on a waiting list. Frequently, when the need is evident, experienced club personnel will help you obtain an instructor and launch a new organization.

In the West the Bonsai Clubs International serves as a coordinator of activities for its member bonsai clubs. A monthly newsletter furnishes hobbyists with announcements of shows and lectures and it carries articles that cover all phases of growing bonsai. For more information address The Editor, *Bonsai*, 2354 Lida Drive, Mountain View, California.

Southern California

Hollywood Bonsai Club. Meeting place: Hollywood Community Center Hall, 3929 Middlebury Street, Los Angeles.

Santa Anita Bonsai Society. Membership by invita-

tion only, for persons experienced in bonsai and with trees to exhibit. Address inquiries to Mrs. Virginia Danaker, 61 East Bonita Avenue, Sierra Madre.

San Fernando Valley Bonsai Club. Meeting place: Japanese-American Community Center, 12953 Branford Street, Pacoima.

San Gabriel Bonsai Club. Meeting place: San Gabriel Community Center, 5019 North Encinita Avenue, Temple City. Address inquiries to Tom Mayeda, 606 East Main Street, San Gabriel.

The following Southern California clubs are for advanced students only. Some have limited memberships.

Baikaen Bonsai Kenkyu Kai. Meeting place: Alpine Baika Bonsai Nursery, 5207 West Jefferson Boulevard, Los Angeles. Address inquiries to Joe Loch, 8180 Mannix Drive, Hollywood.

California Bonsai Society. Meeting place and time arranged by president. Address inquiries to Helen Hart, 934 Third Avenue, Los Angeles.

Santa Ana Bonsai Club. Meeting place: 5314 West Roosevelt Avenue, Santa Ana. Address inquiries to Sam Narasaki at above address.

San Diego Bonsai Society. Meeting place: Floral Building at Balboa Park. Address inquiries to Roy Muroaka, 103 Quintard Street, Chula Vista.

A class (not a club) is open to anyone in the Los Angeles area who would like to attend one or more of its sessions. The instructor is Frank Nagata and the meeting place is Alpine Baika Bonsai Nursery, 5207 West Jefferson Boulevard, Los Angeles.

Hawaii

Hawaii Bonsai Club (Ikeda Chapter). Meeting place: Hilo Electric Light Company Auditorium. Address inquiries to Maseo Kimura, Box 1027, Hilo.

Hilo Bonsai Club. Meeting place: Members' homes in rotation. Address inquiries to Mrs. Jerry Saito, 145 Mauna Kea Street, Hilo.

Honolulu Bonsai Kenkyu Club. Meeting place: Kawahara Nursery, 153 North Kuakini Street, Honolulu. Address inquiries to Tadashi Fukunaga at above address.

Kauai Bonsai Club. Meeting place: Towns in which members reside, in rotation. Address inquiries to Robert M. Oda, Box 222, Koloa, Kauai.

Wahiawa Bonsai Club. Meeting place: Club president's home. Address inquiries to Mrs. Tsuyuko Yano, 1690 California Avenue, Wahiawa.

Northern California

American Bonsai Association. Meeting place: Sacramento Garden and Art Center, 3330 McKinley Blvd., Sacramento. Address inquiries to Donald Croxton, 142 McKiernan Drive, Folsom.

Bonsai Society of San Francisco. Meeting place: Hall of Flowers, Golden Gate Park. Address inquiries to Dr. George Sherman, 69 Cameo Way, San Francisco.

Cascade Bonsai Society. Meeting place: Conference Room, Shasta County Library, 1855 Shasta Street, Redding. Address inquiries to Mrs. Floyd Slack, 3278 Crest Drive, Anderson.

East Bay Bonsai Society. Meeting place: Garden Center, Lakeside Park, Oakland. Address inquiries to Russell Levy, 3639 Butters Drive, Oakland.

Fresno Bonsai Society. Meeting place: Agricultural Department, Fresno State College. Address inquiries to John Roehl, 522 South Cedar, Apartment 6, Fresno.

Kusamura Bonsai Club. Meeting place: Palo Alto Buddhist Church, 2751 Louis Road, Palo Alto. Address inquiries to Thomas Refvem, 112 Stonegate Road, Portola Valley.

Marin Bonsai Club. Meeting place: American Legion Log Cabin, San Anselmo. Address inquiries to Thomas E. Welsh, 675 Hawthorne Drive, Belvedere-Tiburon.

Midori Bonsai Club. Meeting place: Maywood Park, 3330 Pruneridge Road, Santa Clara. Address inquiries to R. C. Miller, 3621 Woodford Drive, San Jose.

Tri-Counties Bonsai Club. Meeting place: Residence of Mrs. Marion Dreyfuss, 20 Creekwood Way, Hillsborough. Address inquiries to Mrs. Helen Levet, 59 Santa Maria, Portola Valley.

The following Northern California clubs are for Japanese speaking students. You might check to see if membership is open to others as well, since things do change.

Fuji Bonsai Club. Meeting place: Buddhist Temple of Berkeley, 2121 Channing Way, Berkeley. Address inquiries to Ricky Sumimoto, 1001 Dwight Way, Berkeley.

Akebono Bonsai Club. Meeting place: Palo Alto Buddhist Church, 2751 Louis Road, Palo Alto. Address inquiries to T. Saburomaru, 1020 Weeks Street, East Palo Alto.

Peninsula Bonsai Club. Meeting place: Palo Alto Buddhist Church, 2751 Louis Road, Palo Alto. Address inquiries to Kenneth Sugimoto, 471 Page Mill Road, Palo Alto.

Pacific Northwest

Kelly Nishitani Bonsai Unit. Meeting place: Arboretum of the University of Washington. Address inquiries to Mrs. Horace Raphael, 2841 Magnolia Boulevard West, Seattle, Washington.

Seattle Bonsai Study Group. Address inquiries to Mrs. Jane Blogg, 814 33rd East, Seattle, Washington.

Midwest and East

Bonsai Society of Michigan. Address inquiries to Mr. Leon Smeltzer, Route 1, Eagle, Michigan.

Cleveland Bonsai Club. Address inquiries to Mrs. Albert M. Baehr, 21708 Avalon Drive, Rocky River, Michigan.

Pennsylvania Bonsai Society. Address inquiries to Mr. William R. Mackinney, 70 N. Middletown Road, Media, Pennsylvania.

Umi-Seashore Area Bonsai Group. Address inquiries to Mrs. George C. Scott, Navesink River Road, Locust, New Jersey.

Bonsai Society of Greater New York. Meeting place: New York Botanical Garden, the Bronx. Address inquiries to Mrs. Mary Case, Box 27, R.D. 1, Bedford Village, New York.

Toronto Bonsai Society. Meeting place: Japanese Canadian Cultural Center, 123 Wynford Drive, Don Mill, Toronto, Canada.

🌲 Seasonal Care Chart

GENUS	PINCHING AND NIPPING	HEAVY PRUNING[1]	WIRING AND BENDING	POTTING AND ROOT PRUNING	FERTILIZING[2]
Abies (Fir)	Spring	Spring-Summer	Any time	Winter-Spring[3]	Winter-Spring
Acer (Maple)	Spring-Summer	Spring-Summer	Spring-Autumn[4]	Winter-Spring	Winter-Spring
Bambusa, Sasa (Bamboo)	Spring-Summer	Spring-Summer	Don't wire	Winter-Spring	Winter-Spring
Camellia (Camellia)	Summer-Winter[5]	Summer-Winter	Summer-Winter	Spring-Summer	Spring-Summer
Cedrus (Cedar)	Spring & Autumn	Any time	Any time	Spring[3]	Winter-Spring
Celtis (Hackberry)	Spring-Summer	Spring-Summer	Spring-Autumn[4]	Winter-Spring	Spring
Chaenomeles (Flowering quince)	Spring-Summer	Spring-Summer	Any time	Winter-Spring	Spring
Chamaecyparis (False cypress)	Spring & Autumn	Any time	Any time	Any time[3]	Winter-Spring
Cornus (Dogwood)	Summer-Winter[5]	Summer	Spring-Autumn[4]	Spring	Spring-Summer
Cotoneaster (Cotoneaster)	Spring-Summer	Spring-Summer	Spring-Summer	Spring-Summer	Winter-Spring[6]
Crataegus (Hawthorn)	Summer[5]	Summer	Spring-Autumn[4]	Spring or Autumn	Spring
Cryptomeria (Cryptomeria)	Spring & Autumn	Spring-Summer	Spring-Summer	Spring-Summer[3]	Winter-Spring
Cupressus (Cypress)	Spring & Autumn	Any time	Any time	Spring-Autumn[3]	Winter-Summer
Diospyros (Persimmon)	Summer-Autumn[5]	Summer	Spring-Autumn[4]	Spring-Summer	Spring-Summer
Fagus (Beech)	Spring-Summer	Spring-Summer	Spring-Summer[4]	Spring	Winter-Spring
Fraxinus (Ash)	Summer-Autumn	Summer-Autumn	Spring-Summer[4]	Spring	Spring
Ginkgo biloba (Maidenhair tree)	Spring-Summer	Spring-Summer	Any time	Winter-Spring	Winter-Spring
Hedera (Ivy)	Spring-Summer	Spring-Summer	Any time	Spring	Winter-Spring
Ilex (Holly)	Spring-Summer	Spring-Summer	Spring-Summer	Winter-Spring	Winter-Spring

THIS CHART SHOWS the best times of the year for carrying out various operations on several representative bonsai genera. Specific plants that do not appear here can usually be fitted into one of the general groups shown. For example, the Maidenhair tree (*Ginkgo biloba*) is a broad-leafed deciduous tree and should be handled in similar manner as the maples (*Acer*).

The four seasons include the months of the year as follows:

Spring: March, April, May.
Summer: June, July, August.
Autumn: September, October, November.
Winter: December, January, February.

When a range of seasons is given, the particular operation can be carried out either late in the former season or early in the latter one. For example, under Potting and Root Pruning, *Acer* is shown Winter-Spring. This means that maples may be repotted any time in February or March.

GENUS	PINCHING AND NIPPING	HEAVY PRUNING	WIRING AND BENDING	REPOTTING AND ROOT PRUNING	FERTILIZING
Jasminum (Jasmine)	Spring & Autumn	Summer-Autumn	Spring-Summer	Spring-Autumn	Winter-Spring
Juniperus (Juniper)	Spring & Autumn	Any time	Any time	Spring[3]	Winter-Spring
Larix (Larch)	Spring & Autumn	Any time	Any time[4]	Winter-Spring	Winter-Spring
Malus (Apple, Flowering crab)	Summer	Summer	Spring-Summer[4]	Spring-Autumn[8]	Spring[9]
Picea (Spruce)	Spring	Spring-Summer	Autumn-Winter	Spring or Autumn[3]	Winter-Spring
Pinus (Pine)	Spring	Summer	Autumn-Winter	Spring or Autumn[3]	Spring
Prunus (Flowering fruits)	Summer-Autumn[5]	Winter-Spring[7]	Spring-Summer[4]	Winter-Spring[10]	Spring[9]
Punica (Pomegranate)	Spring & Autumn	Spring-Summer	Spring-Summer	Spring-Summer	Winter-Spring
Pyracantha (Firethorn)	Spring & Autumn	Spring-Summer	Any time	Spring	Winter-Spring[6]
Quercus (Oak)	Summer-Autumn	Summer-Winter	Spring-Autumn[4]	Spring	Spring
Rhododendron (Azalea)	Summer	Summer	Spring-Summer	Spring-Summer	Spring
Salix (Willow)	Spring-Summer	Summer	Spring-Summer[4]	Spring-Summer	Winter-Spring
Tamarix (Tamarisk)	Spring-Summer	Autumn	Spring-Summer	Spring[3]	Winter-Spring
Taxus (Yew)	Summer	Summer	Summer-Autumn	Spring-Autumn[3]	Spring
Thuja (Arborvitae)	Spring & Autumn	Any time	Any time	Spring[3] or Autumn	Winter-Spring
Tsuga (Hemlock)	Spring & Autumn	Any time	Any time	Spring-Summer[3]	Winter-Spring
Ulmus (Elm)	Spring-Summer	Spring-Summer	Spring-Summer[4]	Winter-Spring	Winter-Spring
Wisteria (Wisteria)	Summer-Winter[5]	Summer-Winter	Spring-Autumn[4]	Spring	Spring
Zelkova serrata (Graybark elm)	Spring-Summer	Spring-Summer	Any time	Winter-Spring	Winter-Spring

Key to Reference Numbers

[1] Feed well one month before pruning any tree.
[2] When winter feeding is noted, this means late winter.
[3] Repot before new shoots open.
[4] Bend after leaves are full size but while branches are still limber.
[5] Trim after flowers die, before new buds harden.

[6] Feed right after fruiting.
[7] Prune after flowering, before leaves appear.
[8] Repot just before flowering.
[9] Feed during flowering.
[10] Repot after flowering, before leaves open.

Index